MATHS & ENGLISH FOR
CONSTRUCTION MULTI-SKILLS

Graduated exercises and practice exam

Andrew Spencer and Gary Taylor

CENGAGE
Learning®

Australia • Brazil • Japan • Korea • Mexico • Singapore • United States

Maths & English for Construction Multi-Skills

Andrew Spencer and Gary Taylor

Publishing Director: Linden Harris

Publisher: Lucy Mills

Development Editor: Claire Napoli

Editorial Assistant: Lauren Darby

Production Editor: Alison Burt

Manufacturing Buyer: Eyvett Davis

Typesetter: Cambridge Publishing
Management Limited

Cover design: HCT Creative

For product information and technology assistance,
contact **emea.info@cengage.com**.

For permission to use material from this text or product,
and for permission queries,
email **emea.permissions@cengage.com**.

This work is adapted from *Pre Apprenticeship: Maths & Literacy Series* by Andrew Spencer published by Cengage Learning Australia Pty Limited © 2010.

British Library Cataloguing-in-Publication Data
A catalogue record for this book is available from the British Library.

ISBN: 978-1-4080-8311-6

Cengage Learning EMEA Cheriton House, North Way, Andover, Hampshire, SP10 5BE United Kingdom

Cengage Learning products are represented in Canada by Nelson Education Ltd.

For your lifelong learning solutions, visit
www.cengage.co.uk

Purchase your next print book, e-book or e-chapter at
www.cengagebrain.com

Printed in Greece by Bakis
1 2 3 4 5 6 7 8 9 10 – 15 14 13

Maths & English for Construction Multi-Skills

Contents

Introduction

It has always been important to understand, from a teacher's perspective, the nature of the mathematical skills students need for their future, rather than teaching them textbook mathematics. This has been a guiding principle behind the development of the content in this workbook. To teach maths and English that is relevant to students seeking apprenticeships is the best that we can do, to give students an education in the field that they would like to work in.

The content in this resource is aimed at the level that is needed for a student to have the best possibility of improving their maths and English skills specifically for trades. Students can use this workbook to prepare for a Functional Skills assessment, or even to assist with basic maths and English for their qualification. This resource has the potential to improve the students' understanding of basic maths concepts that can be applied to trades. These resources have been trialled, and they work.

Commonly used industry terms are introduced so that students have a basic understanding of terminology that they will encounter in the workplace environment. (Words that are in the glossary appear in **bold** the first time they are used.) Students who can complete this workbook and reach a higher outcome in all topics will have achieved the goal of this resource.

The content in this workbook is the first step towards bridging the gap between what has been learnt in previous years, and what needs to be remembered and re-learnt for use in exams and in the workplace. Students will significantly benefit from the consolidation of the basic maths and English concepts.

In many ways, it is a win–win situation, with students enjoying and studying relevant maths and English for work and training organizations and employers receiving students that have improved basic maths and English skills.

All that is needed is patience, hard work, a positive attitude, a belief in yourself that you can do it and a desire to achieve. The rest is up to you.

About the authors

Andrew Spencer has studied education both within Australia and overseas. He has a Bachelor of Education, as well as a Masters of Science in which he specialized in teacher education. Andrew has extensive experience in teaching secondary mathematics throughout New South Wales and South Australia for well over 15 years. He has taught a range of subject areas including Maths, English, Science, Classics, Physical Education and Technical Studies. His sense of the importance of practical mathematics continued to develop with the range of subject areas he has taught in.

This workbook has been adapted by **Gary Taylor**. Gary is a Construction and Engineering curriculum leader at a large college in the North West of England. Gary has over thirty-five years experience in the construction industry, of which twenty years were spent running his own successful company, gaining valuable construction experience. He has taught a range of subjects within the construction industry over the years at various colleges in the North West of England.

Acknowledgements

Andrew Spencer:
 For Paula, Zach, Katelyn, Mum and Dad.
 Many thanks to Mal Aubrey (GTA) and all training organisations for their input.
 Thanks also to the De La Salle Brothers for their selfless support and ongoing work with all students.
 To Dr Pauline Carter for her unwavering support of all Maths teachers.
 This is for all students who value learning, who are willing to work hard and who have character . . .
 and are characters!

Gary Taylor:
 For my wife and best friend Carol for her support over the past thirty years, and to my daughters Rachael and
 Leanne for giving me some wonderful memories over the years.

The publisher would like to thank the many copyright holders who have kindly granted us permission to reproduce material throughout this text. Every effort has been made to contact all rights holders, but in the unlikely event that anything has been overlooked, please contact the publisher directly and we will happily make the necessary arrangements at the earliest opportunity.

ENGLISH

Unit 1 : Spelling

Short-answer questions

Specific instructions to students

- This is an exercise to help you to identify and correct spelling errors.
- Read the activity below, then answer accordingly.

Read the following passage and identify and correct the 20 spelling errors.

> Phil the carpenter arrives on a buillding site at 7.00 a.m. He brings with him everything that he needs for the eight hours of work ahead. The roof needs replasing as do the beems on a small kitchin extension. In addision, the rufters need cheking, the ladder needs setting up and his tool belt needs to be fetched from his work van. The site managor wants the job completed by noon. The aprentice places all of the tools near the site and then uses the tape to begin measureing the job.
>
> At lunch, the carpenter tells the aprentise that a damiged door has to be removed, repared and refited. The apprentise needs to unscrew the hinges with a Phillips-head scew drver. The job also recquires the door to be varnashed and the window has to be taken out of it. Several deep skratches are in the door and it needs cutting back. There was so much work to do that the deadline of noon was impossible and the work would not be able to be complated by the end of the day.

Incorrect words:

_____

_____

Correct words:

_____

_____

Unit 2: Grammar and Punctuation

Short-answer questions

Specific instructions to students

- In this unit, you will be able to practise your grammar and **punctuation** skills.
- Read the activity below, then answer accordingly.

Grammar and Punctuation Task 1 🔵

QUESTION 1

Which linking word or phrase could you use instead of 'whereas'?

Answer:

_____

QUESTION 2

What does the linking word 'alternatively' mean?

Answer:

_____

QUESTION 3

What punctuation is missing from the following **sentence**?

Building maintenance is available to our customers including plastering joinery tiling and all aspects of building maintenance Please contact us for further information

Answer:

_____

_____

QUESTION 4

What is wrong with the following text? Correct the following sentences.

Last week was a very busy week for jack. He had to travel from manchester to london to complete tiling a kitchen. joe the apprentice was great help and the job was finished on time.

Answer:

_____

_____

QUESTION 5

When you have completed a section of writing, what should you look for when checking through your work?

Answer:

_____

_____

QUESTION 6

What is wrong with the following text?

Why not visit our new luxury kitchen showroom set in the heart of rural Lancashire? Youre sure to receive a warm welcome, and be shown the latest models of luxury kitchens that we have available. All our kitchens are very high quality and have a ten year warranty. To find out more or book an appointment, call Andrew on 01435 778367.

Answer:

_____

_____

QUESTION 7

Can you identify the mistake in this job application letter?

Dear Madam

I wish to apply for the vacancy of apprentice joiner, as advertised in this week's Gloucester Globe.

I have just completed my Level 2 NVQ Diploma in Building Maintenance course at Dinsdale Park Colleage and am now looking for work in the Gloucester area.

I enclose a copy of my CV and look forward to hearing from you.

Yours faithfully,

Luke Smith

Answer:

_____

QUESTION 8

Can you identify the mistake in this advert?

Whole House Repairs, West London

Whole House Repairs is set in West London and is a one-stop company for all your house repairs. At Whole House Repairs our highly trained staff will be on hand to insure your every need is catered for.

Please ring 0151 629 40276 to find out more about our special services.

Answer:

_____

_____

Answer:

QUESTION 9

Add **commas** to the following text to make the sense clearer.

Cleaning an oil spill is a very simple task when done correctly. An oil spillage can be very dangerous someone could easily slip on the oil or if there is a large amount it could also be a fire hazard. Spillages should be cleaned up as soon as they happen a small amount of oil can easily be soaked up with an absorbent cloth. If a large oil spillage occurs you should soak it up with absorbent granules. Allow them to soak in for a few hours. When the oil has soaked in sweep the granules up and treat them as **hazardous waste**. They should be stored until you have a large amount and then be collected by a specialist waste company for correct disposal. If the floor still has a greasy feel use some diluted detergent and mop the floor then allow to dry.

Grammar and Punctuation Task 2

Read the following passage and add the appropriate punctuation where necessary.

building tradespersons

building tradespersons jobs include

trowel occupations laying bricks blocks lintels stone and **masonry** walls chimney stacks and archways

plastering finishing off walls inside and outside with plaster cement rendering or pebble dash

tiling fixing ceramic stone marble and limestone tiles to walls and floors

carpentry and joinery making and installing cupboards floorboards roofs doors windows and partitions

roofing tiling slating and flat roof work using felt and asphalt roof sheeting and cladding lead sheeting and sheet metal roofing on industrial buildings

painting painting and decorating on walls floors ceilings and the outside of buildings with masonry paint and other finishes

Answer:

Short-answer questions

Specific instructions to students

- The following exercises are designed to help you understand what you read.

Comprehension Task 1

Read the following passage and answer the questions in sentence form.

Justin the carpenter had to be ready to begin work at 6.30 a.m. on Friday. He arrived at 6.15 a.m. and he knew that the he needed to have most of the work completed by 3.15 p.m. The new apprentice, Joe, arrived at 7.00 a.m. and they both began on the largest job. As Justin knew; the weather would be a major consideration because if it rained, all work would have to cease. The rain would make climbing ladders and working on the roofs difficult and, most importantly, unsafe. Joe climbed the ladder and took with him the nail gun, a claw hammer and 250 roofing nails.

In the meantime, Justin collected some timber **beams** off of the stack that was delivered the day before. He passed Joe four beams and Joe got to work preparing to fit them in place. As he lifted the first beam, Joe felt a pain in his back and he described it as 'a sharp shooting pain that ran down the middle of my back'. Joe stopped work immediately. Justin told him to climb down and they swapped their positions. Justin continued working on the **rafters** while Joe rested. Justin worked quickly as the clouds gathered above them. Joe's back recovered after a short rest and he started to pass the beams to Justin.

At 10.00 a.m. they both took a break to have a drink and something to eat. They were on schedule and things looked good. At 10.25 a.m. Justin and Joe resumed work. They worked well as a team and got most of one side of the house completed. Lunch was at noon and they headed to the local shop to buy something to eat.

They finished lunch at 12.45 p.m. and Justin and Joe began on the other side of the roof. By 1.30 p.m. they were still working very productively, and the roof was looking great. Then, down came the rain. The working day was over at 1.45 p.m. They had no choice but to pack up and go home.

QUESTION 1

Why would rain cause problems on the work site?

Answer:

QUESTION 2

What tools and equipment did Joe take on to the roof with him?

Answer:

QUESTION 3

Why did Joe have to stop work?

Answer:

QUESTION 4

What time did Justin initially want to finish? What time did he actually finish?

Answer:

QUESTION 5

How long was the working day?

Answer:

Comprehension Task 2 (L1) (L2)

Read the following text and answer the questions below.

> The construction industry is very important to all of us. It provides homes, offices, schools, hospitals and **infrastructure** such as roads, power stations, airports and railway stations.
>
> It is important that buildings provide a healthy and pleasant environment, and that they complement the natural surroundings. In the construction industry, advances in materials and design are made every day with new materials and new building techniques. Many of these new techniques conserve energy and reduce the carbon footprint of a building's users.
>
> Construction industry employees of all trades work together in teams for the common goal of completing a contract on time and to their clients' specifications. These teams can include tradespersons, such as plasterers, joiners and carpenters, and a management team who, together with professionals such as architects, designers and inspectors, check that work is carried out safely.

QUESTION 1

Name some categories of building that the construction industry is responsible for.

Answer:

QUESTION 2

What is important about new buildings in the local environment?

Answer:

QUESTION 3

How do new building techniques help the environment?

Answer:

QUESTION 4

Name two tradespersons and two professional people involved in construction?

Answer:

QUESTION 5

What is the common goal of the above construction workers?

Answer:

Comprehension Task 3 (L1) (L2)

Read the following text and answer the questions below.

> The UK construction sector employs over 2 million people and is made up of over 165,000 large, medium and small companies. The large majority of companies are small one-man sole trader firms, making up more than 70% of company profiles. The construction industry can be broken down into three main areas:
>
> - Building and structural engineering
>
> - **Civil engineering**
>
> - Maintenance
>
> **Building and structural engineering** includes the construction of the structure and installation of services for buildings such as factories, offices, shops, leisure centres and houses. Structural engineers are most commonly involved in the design of buildings and large structures, but they can also be involved in the design of any item where structural integrity affects the item's function or safety.
>
> **Civil engineering** is a professional engineering discipline that deals with the design, construction and maintenance of the physical and naturally built environment, including works like bridges, roads, canals, dams, and buildings of every size and shape.
>
> **Maintenance** includes the repair, **refurbishment** and restoration of existing buildings and structures, or services such as water, gas or electricity. Maintenance can therefore be in many forms and disciplines and can also be specialised in various construction activities.

QUESTION 1

How many construction companies (approximately) are there in the UK? And how many people do these companies employ?

Answer:

QUESTION 2

Identify three different categories of construction work in the UK.

Answer:

QUESTION 3

Identify the type of work undertaken in each of the above categories.

Answer:

Comprehension Task 4 Ⓛ1 Ⓛ2

Read the following text from a website and answer the questions below.

Welcome to George Malting (Civil Engineering) Limited

With our head office based on the outskirts of Northampton, George Malting is one of the region's leading civil engineering and groundworks contractors, working on a wide variety of construction projects, from one-off domestic extensions to large housing estates.

Established over forty years ago, we have a strong reputation for quality, reliability and value, and we strive to maintain this. We work closely with our clients to achieve their objectives: meeting their deadlines is a matter of priority, as is working within budgets and maintaining high standards at all times.

We value our relationships with the local community and are proud to be contractors for the local schools, who use our services year after year.

Our project management teams ensure a **risk assessment** is carried out before every project. We recommend energy-saving and **environmentally** friendly products and designs wherever possible, encouraging the three R's of sustainable site design: reduce, reuse, recycle.

QUESTION 1

Is the style of writing formal or informal? Think about what type of language tells you.

QUESTION 2

What is the purpose of this text: is it instructional, informative, persuasive or descriptive?

QUESTION 3

What type of work does this company do?

QUESTION 4

How long has the company been in business?

QUESTION 5

Give two reasons why this seems like a company with a good reputation?

QUESTION 6

Find at least three reasons why this web page is a good advert for the company?

Comprehension Task 5 L1 L2

Read the following text from a blog and answer the questions below.

> Devon Carpentry and Joinery have been established for over thirty years and I've been an apprentice here for nearly a year now, which has given me good experience of different kinds of work. It's a nice working environment, the people are all highly experienced at the job and they're brilliant to learn from. When I first started for the company it took me about forty minutes to do things that now take me ten. My aim is to become a qualified carpenter, but there's a lot to learn and remember. At college I'm working towards getting a Level 2 Carpentry NVQ. Working for Devon Carpentry and Joinery you get to travel around Cornwall and North Devon doing everything from learning how to use circular saws to helping replace rafters.

QUESTION 1

Is the style of writing formal or informal? Think about what type of language tells you.

_____

QUESTION 2

What is the purpose of this text: is it instructional, informative, persuasive or descriptive?

_____

QUESTION 3

How long has this person been an apprentice?

_____

QUESTION 4

Does (s)he enjoy it? How do you know?

_____

QUESTION 5

What is meant by 'nice working environment'?

_____

QUESTION 6

Give three reasons why this apprenticeship is a good one.

_____

Unit 4: Formal Letter Writing Skills

Short-answer questions

Specific instructions to students

- These exercises will help you practise writing formal letters.
- Read the following information on formal letter writing, then write your own letters following the instructions provided.

A formal letter is a method of communication that uses a professional tone and manner. There are many reasons for writing a formal letter. It could be to order supplies, to identify a mistake that was committed or to apologize for an error. A formal letter should be clear, concise and courteous as well as following a set structure. This should include:

- The sender's address.

- Name, title and company name of the addressee.

- Date (day, month and year).

- Heading to indicate the reason for writing the letter.

- Greeting (Dear Mr/Mrs).

- Introductory **paragraph**.

- Middle paragraphs containing the relevant information behind writing the letter.

- Closing paragraph describing what action you expect the recipient to take and a courteous closing sentence.

- A complimentary close ('Yours faithfully' if you wrote 'Dear Sir' or 'Dear Madam' or 'Yours sincerely' if you used the recipient's name).

- Room for your signature.

Section A: Letter of complaint

You have recently purchased a new 18 V cordless drill from a well known supplier. When you first used the drill you notice an intermittent fault with the trigger. When you returned to the place where you bought it, the sales adviser was very dismissive of your concerns and refused to help you. Using the appropriate language, write a letter of complaint to the company's head office, setting out:

- What you purchased

- What is wrong with it

- How you were treated by the sales adviser

- What you would like the company to do to resolve your complaint.

Answer:

Section B: Job application letter

Apprentice Bricklayer / Improver required

Location: Manchester

Salary: £14,000 – rising to £17,000 per annum on qualification

We are currently recruiting for an Apprentice/Improver Bricklayer who has commitment, ambition and real desire to learn about a full range of skills needed to become a professional bricklayer. You will be reporting to the Building Manager, and will be part of a small team working on domestic properties.

The successful applicant must have:

- A quality focus, taking pride in excellent workmanship

- Enthusiasm to work hard

- The ability to work as part of a team.

Please send your application to Mr Andrew Briars, Northern Homes Ltd., Manchester.

You have seen the above advert in your local paper with a vacancy for a trainee. Write a letter of application, setting out why you would like the job and the skills that you have that make you suitable for the job. Continue writing your letter using the notes section at the back of this workbook if required.

Answer:

Short-answer questions

Specific instructions to students

- These exercises will help you practise writing skills that you will need to use when working in the construction industry.
- Complete the writing exercises following the instructions provided.

Section A: Writing emails (L1)

Write an email to your customer, Mr Andrew Richardson, reminding him that you will be starting the work for a new conservatory on the given date.

Answer:

To:

Subject:

Section B: Completing a job record

Fill in all of the sections of this job record for the completed maintenance works on a property owed by your customer Mr Thomas Biggs, 73 Elm Street, Rochdale, Lancashire. His mobile number is 07853 38448678.

CUSTOMER NAME:	DATE:	TIME:

ADDRESS:

TEL HOME:	TEL WORK:
ADDRESS:	JOB NUMBER:

WORK REQUIRED:

WORK CARRIED OUT:

PARTS USED:

ADDITIONAL REPAIRS REQUIRED:

N/A

INVOICE DATE:	INVOICE NO:

CUSTOMER SIGNATURE _____

Section C: Work carried out on a job record

When you write up a job record for the work that has been carried out on a customer's property, it is important to give as much detail as possible. Otherwise the customer may not be charged for all of your work and you in turn could be paid less money.

QUESTION 1

A customer has requested that you paint the front room of a property she is renting out. Give a full write-up of the work carried out.

Answer:

QUESTION 2

Give a full write up of the type of extra work that might be required when working on an older property, where the job has not gone according to plan due to damp plaster and floorboards that are suffering dry rot.

Answer:

QUESTION 3

A customer's property has suffered storm damage. The porch door has been damaged and the double-glazed glass panel needs replacing, along with the gutter outlet. Give a full write-up of works carried out.

Answer:

QUESTION 4

A customer has asked you to carry out extra works while tiling a bathroom. She would now like you to tile the floor in the same room.

Answer:

Section D: Completing a parts invoice

Complete this blank **invoice** for the job activity in question 1 on the previous page. Give the customer a 10% discount and charge VAT at the current rate.

INVOICE

DATE:

INVOICE:

CUSTOMER ID:

BILL TO:

QTY	DESCRIPTION	UNIT	AMOUNT

Item or part description

SUBTOTAL

Description of completed works

SUBTOTAL

OTHER COMMENTS

VAT RATE   %

TAX

DISCOUNT

OTHER

TOTAL DUE

Make all cheques payable to

If you have any questions about this invoice, please contact:

Thank You For Your Business!

Section E: Quotations and estimates

An **estimate** is not a fixed total price and can be amended as work progresses. A quotation is a fixed price and cannot be changed once given. Most tradespersons opt to give estimates for reasons of flexibility. Estimates should include:

- Cost of labour.

- Cost of materials.

- Details of work to be carried out.

- Estimated duration of time to complete the works.

- Any special requirements needed to complete the works.

- Any health and safety issues.

- Full total cost for completed works.

A customer has requested an estimate to replace a plasterboard living room ceiling sized 3 m × 4 m. Using the information detailed above provide a full detailed estimate of the necessary work and cost to replace the ceiling. You can research cost details by using the Internet or suppliers' catalogues.

ESTIMATE

Customer Address:

Estimate details:

Materials needed:

Cost of materials:

Labour charge:

Sub Total:

Vat:

Total:

Signed:

Unit 6: Different Types of Text

Section A: Comparing different types of text (L1) (L2)

Short-answer questions

Specific instructions to students

- This is an exercise to help you identify different types of text.
- Read the activity below, then answer accordingly.

Read each of the following paragraphs, state the purpose of each type of text, explain whether the text is formal or informal and why it is appropriate in this context.

Text A
Dave, can you pick up the materials from Tom's van and then go round to the customer's house and refit the front door. Thanx Raj

Purpose of text:

_____

_____

Formal/informal:

_____

Why the text is appropriate:

_____

_____

_____

Text B
Place a small amount of silicon on to the bottom of the shower screen, using the special silicon gun for this operation. Once the seal is in place, slide the shower screen into place and fix to the tiles with the appropriate supplied screws.

Purpose of text:

_____

_____

Formal/informal:

_____

Why the text is appropriate:

_____

_____

Text C
Please be advised that if this amount of money has not been paid in full, within 30 days of this notice, we will take legal proceedings to recover all of your outstanding debt.

Purpose of text:

_____

_____

Formal/informal:

_____

Why the text is appropriate:

_____

_____

_____

Text D
Work carried out:

- Re-pointed brickwork around front door
- Checked rainwater pipe for leaks
- Painted cast iron gutter above porch.

Purpose of text:

_____

_____

Formal/informal:

_____

Why the text is appropriate:

_____

_____

Section B: Factual and subjective text

Short-answer questions

Specific instructions to students

- This is an exercise to help you identify factual and subjective text.
- Read the activity below, then answer the questions accordingly.

Text can either be factual or subjective.

If a piece of text is factual it is based on real evidence and records of events which is not biased by the writer's opinion.

If a piece of text is subjective, it contains an individual's personal perspective, feelings or opinions which might differ from another individual's view of the same subject.

Which of the following is fact and which is opinion?

QUESTION 1
Liam is the best carpenter that I have ever seen.

_____

QUESTION 2
The new Wembley Stadium has replaced the old Wembley Stadium.

_____

QUESTION 3
I prefer black plastic gutter to brown plastic gutter.

_____

QUESTION 4
My company van is really comfortable on a long journey.

_____

QUESTION 5
The Health and Safety at Work Act was introduced in 1974.

_____

QUESTION 6
You must wear the appropriate **PPE** when you are on a building site.

_____

QUESTION 7
The letters HSAWA stand for the Health and Safety at Work Act.

_____

QUESTION 8
Houses look better when built in red brick than in grey brick.

_____

QUESTION 9
DeWALT make quality work tools.

_____

QUESTION 10
Snap-on make tools for the construction industry.

_____

QUESTION 11
Chrome spanners not only look good, they feel sturdy when you use them.

_____

QUESTION 12
Quotations are a fixed price but estimates can alter during the job.

_____

Section C: Appropriate tone and language

Short-answer questions

Specific instructions to students

- This is an exercise to help you understand the appropriate tone and language to use in text.
- Read the activity below, then answer the question accordingly.

Re-write the letter below to make it more appropriate for its audience. Think specifically about the language, tone and purpose of the text.

For the manager of Top Builders Ltd.

Your builder came to my house to fix a blocked drain. The drain is still not working right and he was very rude. He said the drain was clear and it must be next door's drain causing the blockage. I think he is out of order and will be calling into your office on Friday to get my money back and expect an apology.

From
Thomas Smith

Answer:

Here is an example of an organisation chart for a construction company. Charts like this contain a lot more information than appears at first. The **key** helps you to 'read' the additional information.

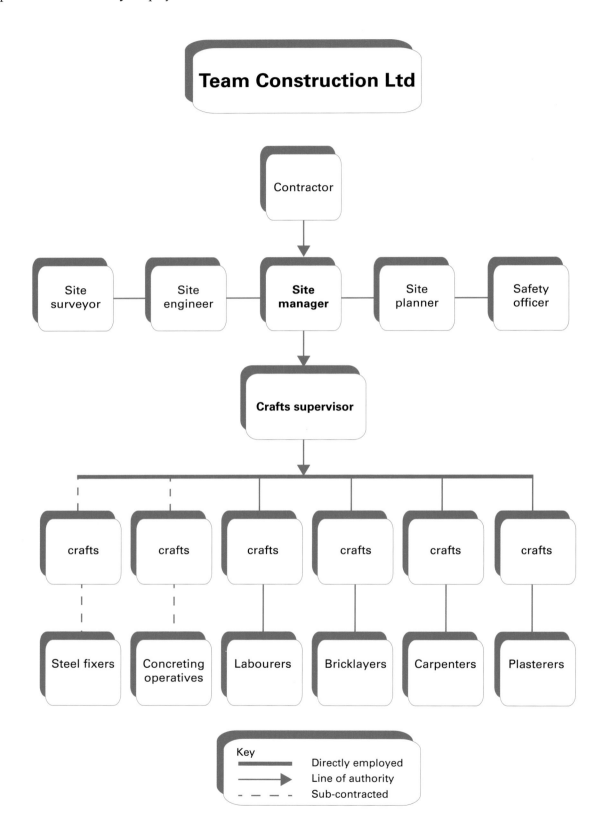

QUESTION 1

Construction projects need a team of people with very different roles and responsibilities to work closely together. To play their part in this, each team member needs to know who they report to. Organisation charts hold a lot of information about the personnel and line management in a company. Use the organisation chart on page 22 to answer these questions.

a List the personnel shown on the example chart who are not directly employed by the company.

Answer:

_____

b List the personnel shown as employed by the company who are on the same level as the site manager.

Answer:

_____

c Number the personnel below in the correct order of line management according to the chart (starting with the employee with most seniority).

Crafts Supervisor   Site Manager   Plasterer

Answer:

_____

_____

QUESTION 2

Read the organisation chart then complete the sentences using an appropriate phrase from the box.

> **is on the same level as**
> **is responsible for**
> **reports to**
> **is responsible to**

a The Crafts Supervisor _____ the Plasterers.

Answer:

_____

b The Safety Officer _____ the Site Manager.

Answer:

_____

c The Crafts Supervisor _____ the Site Manager

Answer:

_____

d The Bricklayers _____ the Crafts Supervisor.

Answer:

_____

QUESTION 3

Use the organisation chart to match the job roles to the job descriptions.

a The _____ manages all of the work on the construction site. This includes managing all personnel, programming and planning.

Answer:

_____

b The _____ supervises the operatives on site.

Answer:

_____

c The _____ 'set out' the location of walls and construct them.

Answer:

_____

d The _____ is usually responsible for 'setting out' the exact position of all buildings, roads and drains.

Answer:

_____

e The _____ is in charge of making sure that all construction operations on site meet the requirement of health and safety legislation.

Answer:

_____

MATHEMATICS

It is important to show your workings out to indicate how you calculated your answer. Use this workbook to practice the questions and record your answers. Use the blank Notes pages at the back of the book to record your workings out.

Unit 8: General Mathematics

Short-answer questions

Specific instructions to students

- This unit will help you to improve your general mathematical skills.
- Read the questions below and answer all of them in the spaces provided.
- You need to show all working, you can use the blank Notes pages at the back of this book.

QUESTION 1

What unit of measurement would you use to measure:

a   The length of a piece of skirting board?

Answer:

_____

b   The total **area** of a room?

Answer:

_____

c   The amount of glue in a hot glue gun?

Answer:

_____

d   The weight of a roof truss?

Answer:

_____

e   The speed of a vehicle?

Answer:

_____

f   The amount of antifreeze in a fuel?

Answer:

_____

g   The cost of a hammer drill?

Answer:

_____

QUESTION 2

Give examples of how the following might be used in the building industry.

a   **Percentages**

Answer:

_____

b   **Decimals**

Answer:

_____

c   **Fractions**

Answer:

_____

_____

d   Mixed numbers

Answer:

_____

_____

e   **Ratios**

Answer:

_____

f   Angles

Answer:

_____

QUESTION 3
Convert the following units.

a   1.2 m to both centimetres and millimetres

Answer:

_____

b   4 tonnes to kilograms

Answer:

_____

c   260 cm to millimetres

Answer:

_____

d   1140 ml to litres

Answer:

_____

e   1650 g to kilograms

Answer:

_____

f   1.8 kg to grams

Answer:

_____

g   3 m to both centimetres and millimetres

Answer:

_____

h   4.5 litres to millilitres

Answer:

_____

QUESTION 4
Write the following in descending order:

0.4   0.04   4.1   40.0   400.00   4.0

Answer:

_____

QUESTION 5
Write the decimal number that is half-way between:

a   0.2 and 0.4

Answer:

_____

b   1.8 and 1.9

Answer:

_____

c   12.4 and 12.5

Answer:

_____

d   28.3 and 28.4

Answer:

_____

e   101.5 and 101.7

Answer:

_____

QUESTION 6
Round off the following numbers to two (2) decimal places.

a   12.346

Answer:

_____

b   2.251

Answer:

_____

c   123.897

Answer:

_____

d   688.882

Answer:

_____

e   1209.741

Answer:

_____

QUESTION 7

Estimate the following using approximation.

a $1288 \times 19 =$

Answer:

_____

b $201 \times 20 =$

Answer:

_____

c $497 \times 12.2 =$

Answer:

_____

d $1008 \times 10.3 =$

Answer:

_____

e $399 \times 22 =$

Answer:

_____

f $201 - 19 =$

Answer:

_____

g $502 - 61 =$

Answer:

_____

h $1003 - 49 =$

Answer:

_____

i $10\,001 - 199 =$

Answer:

_____

j $99.99 - 39.8 =$

Answer:

_____

QUESTION 8

What do the following add up to?

a   £4.00, £4.99 and £144.95

Answer:

_____

b   8.75, 6.9 and 12.55

Answer:

_____

c   650 mm, 1800 mm and 2290 mm

Answer:

_____

d   21.3 mm, 119.8 mm and 884.6 mm

Answer:

_____

QUESTION 9

Subtract the following.

a   2338 from 7117

Answer:

_____

b   1786 from 3112

Answer:

_____

c   5979 from 8014

Answer:

_____

d   11\,989 from 26\,221

Answer:

_____

e   108\,767 from 231\,111

Answer:

_____

QUESTION 10

Solve the following.

a $2177 \div 7$

Answer:

_____

b $4484 \div 4$

Answer:

_____

c $63.9 \div 0.3$

Answer:

_____

d $121.632 \div 1.2$

Answer:

_____

e $466.88 \div 0.8.$

Answer:

_____

The following information is provided for Question 11.

To solve using BODMAS, in order from left to right, solve the Brackets first, then Order ('to the power of'), then Division, then Multiplication, then Addition and lastly Subtraction. The following example has been done for your reference.

EXAMPLE

Solve $(4 \times 7) \times 2 + 6 - 4.$

_____

STEP 1

Solve the Brackets first: $(4 \times 7) = 28$

STEP 2

No Division, so next solve Multiplication: $28 \times 2 = 56$

STEP 3

Addition is next: $56 + 6 = 62$

STEP 4

Subtraction is the last process: $62 - 4 = 58$

_____

FINAL ANSWER:

_____

QUESTION 11

Using BODMAS, solve:

a $(6 \times 9) \times 5 + 7 - 2 =$

Answer:

_____

b $(9 \times 8) \times (4 + 6) - 1 =$

Answer:

_____

c $3 \times 5 \times (7 + 11) - 8 =$

Answer:

_____

d $6 + (9 + 5 \times 8) \div 7 =$

Answer:

_____

e $(9 - 7) + 6 \times (3 + 9) \times 2^2 =$

Answer:

_____

f $2 \times (4 + 5^2) - (8 - 4) =$

Answer:

_____

Section A: Addition

Short-answer questions

Specific instructions to students

- This section will help you to improve your addition skills for basic operations.
- Read the following questions and answer all of them in the spaces provided.
- You need to show all working, you can use the blank Notes pages at the back of this book.

QUESTION 1

A carpenter uses four lengths of 75 mm × 25 mm oak measuring 2 m, 1 m, 3 m and 5 m. How much wood does he use in total?

Answer:

QUESTION 2

To renovate a house a carpenter uses four lengths of floorboard that measure 2.5 m, 1.8 m, 3.3 m and 15.2 m. How much wood does she use in total?

Answer:

QUESTION 3

A builders' merchant stocks 2170 of 10 cm galvanised nails, 368 of 8 cm galvanized nails and 723 various galvanised nails. How many nails do they have in stock in total?

Answer:

QUESTION 4

Over four weeks, a carpenter travels 282 miles, 344 miles, 489 miles and 111 miles respectively. How far has the carpenter travelled in total over the four weeks?

Answer:

QUESTION 5

A builder uses the following amounts of fascia board over a month: 32 m in week one; 47 m in week two; 57 m in week three; and 59 m in week four. How much fascia board has been used in total?

Answer:

QUESTION 6

An apprentice joiner buys a hammer for £22, 4 screwdrivers for £16 and a tape measure for £9. How much has been spent in total?

Answer:

QUESTION 7

Tom the joiner uses 8 cm galvanized nails to complete three jobs on a building site: 86 are used on one job, 132 on another and 97 on the last job. How many have been used in total?

Answer:

QUESTION 8

A cabinet maker buys a lathe for £1589.00, a drill for £169.00 and a circular saw for £209.00. How much has been spent in total?

Answer:

QUESTION 9

The floors of a restaurant that is being renovated need new timber to replace floorboards that are worn. If 16 m are used for one room, 18 m for another, 8 m for another and 11 m for the last room, how much timber has been used in total?

Answer:

QUESTION 10

To complete some carpentry work, 178 galvanised nails, 188 tacks and 93 wood screws are needed. How many fixings in total are used?

Answer:

Section B: Subtraction

Short-answer questions

Specific instructions to students

- This section will help you to improve your addition skills for basic operations.
- Read the following questions and answer all of them in the spaces provided.
- You need to show all working, you can use the blank Notes pages at the back of this book.

QUESTION 1

The company van is filled to the limit with 52 litres of petrol on Wednesday. If 12 litres are used on Friday, 13 litres are used on Saturday and 11 litres are used on Sunday, how much petrol remains in the tank for work on Monday?

Answer:

QUESTION 2

A cabinet maker has a pack of 500 wood screws. If 244 screws are used in November and 137 screws are used during December, how many screws are left for use in January?

Answer:

QUESTION 3

If apprentice carpenter Freya uses 243 m of timber on several jobs and her partner Haz uses 159 m of timber on different jobs, how much more timber has Freya used than Haz?

Answer:

QUESTION 4

Armin the wall tiler uses 72 tiles out a box that originally contained 250 tiles. How many tiles are left in the box?

Answer:

QUESTION 5

Joe the painter and decorator, charges £230.00 to redecorate a bedroom. If Joe gives the customer a discount of £27.00, how much does the customer need to pay?

Answer:

QUESTION 6

A wood yard manager orders 5000 m of pine. Over 6 months, 2756 m of the pine is sold. How much pine remains?

Answer:

QUESTION 7

The area of a storeroom totals 96 m². If 44 m² are used to store timber and 17 m² are used to store tools, how much room, in square metres, remains?

Answer:

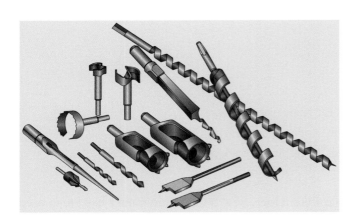

QUESTION 8

A builder replaces his drill bits 69 times over a year. If he had a total of 105 drill bits to begin with, how many have not been replaced?

Answer:

QUESTION 9

A company van has a mileage reading of 56 089 miles at the start of the year. At the end of the year the mileage reads 71 101 miles. How many miles have been travelled in the year?

Answer:

QUESTION 10

A roof tiler uses 31 galvanized nails on one job, 29 galvanized nails on another job and 103 galvanized nails on the last job. If there were 250 galvanized nails to begin with, how many galvanized nails are now left?

Answer:

Section C: Multiplication

Short-answer questions

Specific instructions to students

- This section will help you to improve your multiplication skills for basic operations.
- Read the following questions and answer all of them in the spaces provided.
- You need to show all working, you can use the blank Notes pages at the back of this book.

QUESTION 1

A master builder charges £40 per hour. How much does he earn for a 45-hour week?

Answer:

QUESTION 2

If a cabinet maker uses 14 wood screws to construct a cabinet, how many would be needed to construct 15 more identical cabinets?

Answer:

QUESTION 3

A builder uses 13 litres of diesel for one trip to a work site. How much fuel is used if the builder works on the site for 18 days and does the same trip each day?

Answer:

_____

QUESTION 4

A builder uses 12 nuts, 12 bolts and 24 washers on one job. How many nuts, bolts and washers would be used on 24 more identical jobs?

Answer:

_____

QUESTION 5

A carpenter uses three lengths of oak for one job, 1.5 m, 2.2 m and 0.8 m. How many metres of oak would be used for 39 more identical jobs?

Answer:

_____

QUESTION 6

Amanda, an apprentice joiner, uses 16 wood screws to hang one fire door. How may screws would she need to hang 87 more fire doors?

Answer:

_____

QUESTION 7

A company van uses 9 litres of petrol for every 100 miles travelled. How much petrol would be used to travel 450 miles?

Answer:

_____

QUESTION 8

If a cabinet maker used 673 wood screws per month, how many would be used over one year?

Answer:

_____

QUESTION 9

Mark, an apprentice plasterer, uses 8 m of skim bead each day. How much is used during a month of 31 days?

Answer:

_____

QUESTION 10

If a company van travels at 65 miles per hour (mph), how far will the van have travelled after 5 hours?

Answer:

_____

Section D: Division

Short-answer questions

Specific instructions to students

- This section will help you to improve your division skills for basic operations.
- Read the following questions and answer all of them in the spaces provided.
- You need to show all working, you can use the blank Notes pages at the back of this book.

QUESTION 1

An apprentice plasterer has 24 m of ceiling coving delivered to site. How many jobs can be completed if each standard job requires 3m of coveing?

Answer:

_____

QUESTION 2

Paul the bricklayer earns £868.00 for working a five-day week. How much is earned on average per day?

Answer:

_____

QUESTION 3

A painter and decorator buys 140 litres of wood varnish in bulk before pouring it into 4 litres containers.

a How many containers will be filled?

Answer:

b Will any varnish be left over?

Answer:

QUESTION 4

Ryan the builder carries out maintenance on numerous properties. If he travels 780 miles in a 5-day week, on average how many miles per day have been travelled?

Answer:

QUESTION 5

The total weight of a specially designed oak table is 88 kg. How much load, in kilograms, is on each of the 4 legs?

Answer:

QUESTION 6

A builder uses 2925 m of 3 × 2 scant on 7 different jobs. How many metres are used on each job?

Answer:

QUESTION 7

At a yearly stocktake, a storeman at a large building company counts 2326 wood screws.

a If 100 screws fit into a box, how many full boxes of screws are there?

Answer:

b Are any screws left over?

Answer:

QUESTION 8

A ceramic wall tiling company business tops up its supplies by ordering in 408 packets of plastic tile spacers. If these packets are stored in boxes of six, how many boxes will be needed?

Answer:

QUESTION 9

A truck delivers 645 m of pine to a furniture company. The wood is to be used for making table legs.

a If each leg measures 800 mm, how many legs could be made from the pine?

Answer:

b Is any wood left over?

Answer:

QUESTION 10

A company contracts manager travels 3890 miles over 28 days while inspecting work sites. How many miles are travelled each day on average?

Answer:

Unit 10: Decimals

Section A: Addition L1 L2

Short-answer questions

Specific instructions to students

- This section will help you to improve your addition skills when working with decimals.
- Read the following questions and answer all of them in the spaces provided.
- You need to show all working, you can use the blank Notes pages at the back of this book.

QUESTION 1

If you buy 4 sets of screwdrivers for a total of £137.99 and a claw hammer for £22.75, how much will you spend in total?

Answer:

QUESTION 2

An apprentice carpenter buys a drill for £39.95; a set of drill bits for £29.95; several hole-saws for £44.55; and a set of clamps for £19.45. How much has she spent in total?

Answer:

QUESTION 3

Three lengths of beading measure 29.85 m, 19.50 m and 15.65 cm. What is the total length of beading?

Answer:

QUESTION 4

One length of drainage pipe measures 1105.5 cm and another length measures 988.5 cm. What is the total length of both pieces of pipe?

Answer:

QUESTION 5

An apprentice joiner buys the following for work: a clamp for £8.99; a set of hinges for £6.50; a packet of screws for £6.50; and a door lock for £25.99. What is the total cost?

Answer:

QUESTION 6

Sara the company surveyor travels 65.8 miles, 35.5 miles, 22.7 miles and 89.9 miles, how far has she travelled in total?

Answer:

QUESTION 7

What is the total length of a wood chisel with a handle measuring 5.5 cm and an end of 7.8 cm?

Answer:

QUESTION 8

Two sheets of medium-density fireboard (MDF) are fitted side by side. If the side of one sheet measures 242.5 cm and the side of the other sheet measures 379.5 cm, what is the combined length of both sides?

Answer:

QUESTION 9

A plasterer completes three jobs: £450.80 is charged for the first job; £1130.65 for the second job; and £660.45 for the last job. How much has been charged in total?

Answer:

_____

QUESTION 10

One side of a tool box has a length of 89.90 cm. What is the distance around the **perimeter** if all 4 sides are of equal length?

Answer:

_____

Section B: Subtraction

Short-answer questions

Specific instructions to students

- This section will help you to improve your subtraction skills when working with decimals.
- Read the following questions and answer all of them in the spaces provided.
- You need to show all working, you can use the blank Notes pages at the back of this book.

QUESTION 1

From a 2 m length of plasterboard, a plasterer cuts two lengths for a ceiling. If the the two pieces measure 388 mm and 295 mm, how much of the original length, in millimetres, remains?

Answer:

_____

QUESTION 2

If a builder uses a circular saw to cut a 225 mm length from a beam that is 1450 mm long, what is the length of the beam after it is cut?

Answer:

_____

QUESTION 3

An apprentice wall tiler completes a job tiling a bathroom that costs £789.20. Her boss then gives the customer a discount of £75.50. How much is the final cost after the discount?

Answer:

_____

QUESTION 4

A painter and decorator works for 38 hours and earns a total of £245.60. After receiving his wages, he goes to the petrol station and fills the tank of his car with petrol. If the petrol costs £48.85, how much money does he have left?

Answer:

_____

QUESTION 5

Scaffolding is used to reach an area of the outside of a house that is 3.60 m high. The scaffolding then needs to be lowered to a height of 2.95 m to work on the next section of the house. How far down does it need to be lowered?

Answer:

_____

QUESTION 6

Timber is delivered to a building site. Two lengths need to be cut from a 6 m length. The two lengths measure 2250 mm and 2870 mm respectively. How much is left from the original 6 m length?

Answer:

_____

QUESTION 7

If two 1550 mm lengths of door **casing** are cut from a 4 m length, how much door casing is left?

Answer:

_____

QUESTION 8

A length of timber measures 1250 mm. If a length of 900 mm is cut from it, how much timber remains?

Answer:

_____

QUESTION 9

A builder has a 5 m length of plywood. It is used for three different jobs: 1850 mm for job 1; 1650 mm for job 2; and 950 mm for job 3. How much plywood is left?

Answer:

_____

QUESTION 10

A builder has a 2 m length of soffit board. If 350 mm is used on one job and then 765 mm and 445 mm are used on two other jobs, how much soffit board is left?

Answer:

_____

Section C: Multiplication (L1) (L2)

Short-answer questions

Specific instructions to students

- This section will help you to improve your multiplication skills when working with decimals.
- Read the following questions and answer all of them in the spaces provided.
- You need to show all working, you can use the blank Notes pages at the back of this book.

QUESTION 1

A 4-litre can of varnish costs £19.95. To complete a job, a painter and decorator needs 5 cans of the varnish. How much will the varnish cost in total?

Answer:

_____

QUESTION 2

One litre of varnish costs £5.50. If an apprentice purchases 16 litres of varnish, what is the total cost?

Answer:

_____

QUESTION 3

A cabinet maker replaces 6 pairs of cupboard doors at a cost of £64.50 each. What is the total cost of the replacement doors?

Answer:

_____

QUESTION 4

If a builder uses 6 packets of wood screws that cost £8.65 per packet, how much do the screws cost in total?

Answer:

QUESTION 5

An apprentice buys 12 rawl bolts that cost £1.95 each. How much do the bolts cost in total?

Answer:

QUESTION 6

A master builder earns £43.50 per hour. If he works 50 hours in one week, what is his gross wage (before tax)?

Answer:

QUESTION 7

A furniture workshop buys wood for £2.55 per metre. If 25 m are purchased, how much was spent in total?

Answer:

QUESTION 8

A builder's car has a 52-litre tank. Fuel costs £1.95 per litre. How much would the builder have to pay to fill the tank?

Answer:

QUESTION 9

A company manager purchases 3400 m of pine for £2.15 per metre. What is the total outlay?

Answer:

QUESTION 10

A carpenter earns £220.65 per day. What is her gross weekly wage (before tax) for 5 days?

Answer:

Section D: Division

Short-answer questions

Specific instructions to students

- This section will help you to improve your division skills when working with decimals.
- Read the following questions and answer all of them in the spaces provided.
- You need to show all working, you can use the blank Notes pages at the back of this book.

QUESTION 1

An apprentice has 28.5 litres of varnish that is to be used on 6 separate jobs. How much needs to be allocated for each job if each job needs the same amount of varnish?

Answer:

QUESTION 2

A joiner earns £990.60 for 5 days of work. How much is earned per day?

Answer:

QUESTION 3

A builder charges £3732.70 to complete some work on a house. If it takes 70 hours to complete the job, what is the hourly rate?

Answer:

QUESTION 4

A plasterer completes a job worth £540.85 that takes 16 hours. What is the hourly rate?

Answer:

QUESTION 5

Martin the wall tiler drives from Lancashire to Cumbria to tile a kitchen, and travels 380 miles in five days. How far has been travelled, on average each day?

Answer:

QUESTION 6

A builder wins a contract in London. He needs to drive from Manchester to London and travels 297 miles to reach the job. The trip takes 5.5 hours to complete. How far has been travelled, on average, per hour?

Answer:

QUESTION 7

A company van uses 36 litres of diesel to travel 575.8 miles. How far does the van travel per litre?

Answer:

QUESTION 8

A woodworking workshop buys 36 spanner sets at a cost of £890. How much does one set cost?

Answer:

QUESTION 9

It costs £85.80 to fill a 52-litre fuel tank. How much is the cost of fuel per litre?

Answer:

QUESTION 10

A painter buys 3 different sizes of paint brushes totalling £18.60. How much does each paint brush cost if they are the same unit price?

Answer:

Section A: Addition

Short-answer questions

Specific instructions to students

- This section will help you to improve your addition skills when working with fractions.
- Read the following questions and answer all of them in the spaces provided.
- You need to show all working, you can use the blank Notes pages at the back of this book.

QUESTION 1

$\frac{1}{2} + \frac{4}{5} =$

Answer:

_____

QUESTION 2

$2\frac{1}{2} + 1\frac{2}{3} =$

Answer:

_____

QUESTION 3

A carpenter pours $\frac{1}{3}$ of a bottle of PVC glue into a container. Another $\frac{1}{4}$ of a bottle of PVC glue is added from another bottle. How much glue is there now in the container in total? Express your answer as a fraction.

Answer:

_____

QUESTION 4

One can of varnish $\frac{1}{3}$ full. Another can is $\frac{1}{2}$ full. How much varnish is there in total? Express your answer as a fraction.

Answer:

_____

QUESTION 5

A painter has $1\frac{2}{3}$ cans of varnish. $1\frac{1}{4}$ of another can of varnish is added. How much varnish is there in total? Express your answer as a fraction.

Answer:

_____

Section B: Subtraction

Short-answer questions

Specific instructions to students

- This section will help you to improve your subtraction skills when working with fractions.
- Read the following questions and answer all of them in the spaces provided.
- You need to show all working, you can use the blank Notes pages at the back of this book.

QUESTION 1

$\frac{2}{3} - \frac{1}{4} =$

Answer:

_____

QUESTION 2

$2\frac{2}{3} - 1\frac{1}{4} =$

Answer:

_____

QUESTION 3

A joiner has a can of wood varnish that is $\frac{2}{3}$ full. $\frac{1}{2}$ of the can is used as a finish on a dining table. How much varnish is left? Express your answer as a fraction.

Answer:

_____

QUESTION 4

A wood machinist uses oil on two lathes. If there is $\frac{3}{4}$ of a can to begin with, and he uses $\frac{1}{3}$ of a can, what fraction is left?

Answer:

_____

QUESTION 5

A builder has $2\frac{1}{2}$ litres of PVC glue. If $1\frac{1}{3}$ litres are used for one job, how much glue is left as a fraction?

Answer:

_____

Section C: Multiplication

Short-answer questions

Specific instructions to students

- This section will help you to improve your multiplication skills when working with fractions.
- Read the following questions and answer all of them in the spaces provided.
- You need to show all working, you can use the blank Notes pages at the back of this book.

QUESTION 1

Solve $\frac{2}{4} \times \frac{2}{3}$

Answer:

QUESTION 2

$2\frac{2}{3} \times 1\frac{1}{2} =$

Answer:

QUESTION 3

A carpenter wants to build a flight of stairs that will have 15 steps in it. What is the total vertical height from the floor to the top of the staircase if each step is $16\frac{1}{2}$ cm high?

Answer:

QUESTION 4

A builder has an $8\frac{1}{2}$ m beam that needs to be cut to $\frac{3}{4}$ of its length. What will the new length measure?

Answer:

QUESTION 5

An apprentice needs to build a 13-step flight of stairs. The height of each step measures $18\frac{1}{2}$ cm. What will be the total vertical height from the floor to the top?

Answer:

Section D: Division

Short-answer questions

Specific instructions to students

- This section will help you to improve your division skills when working with fractions.
- Read the following questions and answer all of them in the spaces provided.
- You need to show all working, you can use the blank Notes pages at the back of this book.

QUESTION 1

$\frac{2}{3} \div \frac{1}{4} =$

Answer:

_____

QUESTION 2

$2\frac{3}{4} \div 1\frac{1}{3} =$

Answer:

_____

QUESTION 3

A builder has to put new floorboards in a room that is $3\frac{1}{2}$ m wide. How many floorboards will need to be cut, if each floorboard measures 25 cm wide? (Remember to convert from centimetres into metres.)

Answer:

_____

QUESTION 4

The vertical height of a staircase measures $2\frac{3}{4}$ m. What is the height of each step if 16 steps are required for the staircase?

Answer:

_____

QUESTION 5

A carpenter wants to fit wall panelling across a wall that measures $2\frac{1}{2}$ m. If each panel measures 250 mm, how many are needed? (Hint: Make sure you work in the same units.)

Answer:

_____

Unit 12: Percentages

Short-answer questions

Specific instructions to students

- In this unit, you will be able to practise and improve your skills in working out percentages.
- Read the following questions and answer all of them in the spaces provided.
- You need to show all working, you can use the blank Notes pages at the back of this book.

10% rule: move the digits one place to the right to get 10%. This has the effect of moving the decimal point one place to the left.

EXAMPLE

10% of £45.00 would be £4.50

QUESTION 1

A builder repairs a floor at a cost of £5220.00. The builder then gives his client a discount of 10%.

a How much does the discount work out to in pounds?

Answer:

_____

b What is the final cost to the client?

Answer:

_____

QUESTION 2

A nail gun costs £249.00 at a tool shop. The shop then has a sale, and the nail gun is given a 10% discount.

a How much does the discount work out to in pounds?

Answer:

_____

b What will the final price of the nail gun be after the 10% is taken off?

Answer:

_____

QUESTION 3

The manager of a woodwork workshop sees a 2 hp portable air conditioning unit on sale for £698.00. After negotiating with a sales assistant, a 10% discount is given. How much will the air conditioning unit cost? (Hint: find 10% and subtract it from the cost of the air conditioner.)

Answer:

_____

QUESTION 4

An apprentice painter and decorator buys 5 litres of thinners for £24.60. She gets a 5% discount. How much does this reduce the price? What is the final price? (Hint: find 10%, halve it and then subtract it from £24.60.)

Answer:

_____

QUESTION 5

A builder buys 3 packets of sandpaper that total to £20, a 14 V cordless drill for £69 and 2 sanding blocks that come to £10.50.

a How much is paid in total?

Answer:

_____

b How much is paid after a 10% discount?

Answer:

_____

QUESTION 6

The following items are purchased for a builders' merchant: a fluorescent work light for £19.99; a sanding disc for £9.99, a set of chisels for £89.99, a packet of marking pencils for £6.99 and a 15 m extension lead for £14.99.

a What is the total cost of all the items?

Answer:

b What is the final cost after a 10% discount?

Answer:

QUESTION 7

A tool shop offers 20% off of the price of screwdriver sets. If a set is priced at £26 before the discount, how much will they cost after the discount?

Answer:

QUESTION 8

Cordless drills are discounted by 15%. If the regular retail price is £65.00 each, what is the discounted price?

Answer:

QUESTION 9

The regular retail price of a set of chisels is £56.00. If the store has a 20% sale of all items, how much will the chisel set cost during the sale?

Answer:

QUESTION 10

An 18-**volt** impact driver retails at £99.00. How much will it cost after the store manager takes 30% off?

Answer:

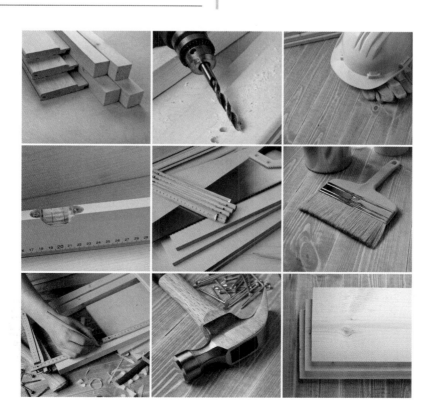

Unit 13: Measurement Conversions

Short-answer questions

Specific instructions to students

- This unit is designed to help you to both improve your skills and to increase your speed in converting one measurement unit into another.
- Read the following questions and answer all of them in the spaces provided.
- You need to show all working, you can use the blank Notes pages at the back of this book.

QUESTION 1

How many millimetres are there in 1 cm?

Answer:

QUESTION 2

How many centimetres are there in 1 m?

Answer:

QUESTION 3

How many millimetres are there in 1 m?

Answer:

QUESTION 4

After plastering a living room, Dave the plasterer has 2550 mm of skrim left over. How long is it in metres?

Answer:

QUESTION 5

The length of a floor **joist** measures 3650 mm. How long is it in metres?

Answer:

QUESTION 6

A piece of roofing felt measures 2.6m. How long will it measure in millimetres?

Answer:

QUESTION 7

Two lengths of hardwood measure 285 cm and 325 cm. What is the total length, in millimetres, when the two are added?

Answer:

QUESTION 8

A carpenter needs three separate lengths of maple to complete a job. The lengths measure 2.45 m, 3.15 m and 1.85 m. What is the total length in millimetres?

Answer:

QUESTION 9

A builder uses four lengths of old English oak that measure 2580 mm, 3250 mm, 4200 mm and 4400 mm. How much does this measure in total, in metres?

Answer:

QUESTION 10

An apprentice joiner has 12 m of skirting board. From this, 5 lengths are cut: 1850 mm, 1350 mm, 1380 mm, 2100 mm and 2350 mm.

a How long are the 5 lengths put together? State your answer in metres.

Answer:

b How much is left from the original skirting board? Give your answer in metres.

Answer:

Section A: Circumference L1 L2

Short-answer questions

Specific instructions to students

- This section is designed to help you both to improve your skills and to increase your speed in measuring the **circumference** of a round object.
- Read the following questions and answer all of them in the spaces provided.
- You need to show all working, you can use the blank Notes pages at the back of this book.
- Give your answers to a suitable level of accuracy.

$C = \pi \times d$

where: C = circumference, $\pi = 3.14$, d = diameter

EXAMPLE

Find the circumference of a sanding disc with a **diameter** of 150 mm.

$C = \pi \times d$

Therefore, $C = 3.14 \times 150$

$= 471$ mm

The diameter $= 2 \times$ the radius

QUESTION 1

Calculate the circumference of a round table with a diameter of 900 mm.

Answer:

_____

QUESTION 2

Find the circumference of a cement mixer drum with a diameter of 145 mm.

Answer:

_____

QUESTION 3

Determine the circumference of a hole for a kitchen light with a diameter of 120 mm.

Answer:

_____

QUESTION 4

Find the circumference of the top of a wooden table with a diameter of 16 cm.

Answer:

_____

QUESTION 5

Calculate the circumference of a round plasterer's bucket with a radius of 6 cm.

Answer:

_____

QUESTION 6

Find the circumference of a bathroom fan with a diameter of 18 cm.

Answer:

_____

QUESTION 7

Calculate the circumference of a round bathroom mirror with a diameter of 130 cm.

Answer:

_____

QUESTION 8

Find the circumference of a circular power saw with a radius of 12 cm.

Answer:

_____

QUESTION 9

Determine the circumference of a sanding disc with a diameter of 14 cm.

Answer:

_____

QUESTION 10

Find the circumference of an orbital sander with a diameter of 17 cm.

Answer:

_____

Section B: Diameter

$$\text{Diameter (D) of a circle} = \frac{\text{circumference}}{\pi(3.14)}$$

EXAMPLE

Find the diameter of a cooking pot with a circumference of 80 mm.

$$D = \frac{80}{\pi(3.14)} = 25.48 \text{ mm} = 25 \text{ mm (nearest mm)}$$

QUESTION 1

Find the diameter of an orbital sander with a circumference of 24 cm.

Answer:

_____

QUESTION 2

Calculate the diameter of a round hole in a wall for a window with a circumference of 628 cm.

Answer:

_____

QUESTION 3

Find the diameter of a round window hole in a door with a circumference of 200 mm.

Answer:

_____

QUESTION 4

Determine the diameter of a hole made by a hole-saw with a circumference of 130 mm.

Answer:

_____

QUESTION 5

Find the diameter of a bored hole with a circumference of 43 mm.

Answer:

_____

QUESTION 6

Determine the diameter of a round fire stop spacer with a circumference of 84 cm.

Answer:

_____

QUESTION 7

Find the diameter of a round grinding disc with a circumference of 12.4 cm.

Answer:

_____

QUESTION 8

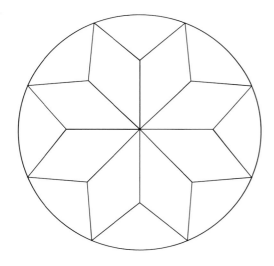

Calculate the diameter of a circular wooden template with a circumference of 90.8 cm.

Answer:

_____

QUESTION 9

Find the diameter of a diamond core drill with a circumference of 62.3 cm.

Answer:

_____

QUESTION 10

Calculate the diameter of a round drain rodding eye with a circumference of 68.8 cm.

Answer:

_____

Section C: Area

Short-answer questions

Specific instructions to students

- This section is designed to help you both to improve your skills and to increase your speed in measuring surface area.
- Read the following questions and answer all of them in the spaces provided.
- You need to show all working, you can use the blank Notes pages at the back of this book.

> Area = length × width
> = *l* × *w*
> and is given in square units

QUESTION 1

If the measurements of the base of a builder's tool box are 40 cm long by 21 cm wide, what is the total area?

Answer:

QUESTION 2

A joiner has to order enough laminated floor to cover a room 60m by 13m. How much laminated flooring is needed to be ordered to cover the floor area?

Answer:

QUESTION 3

If a sheet of plywood measures 2.85 m by 1.65 m, what is its total area?

Answer:

QUESTION 4

The front of a wooden door measures 2.1 m by 0.8 m. What is the door's total area?

Answer:

QUESTION 5

A joiner purchases a 3 m × 1.5 m sheet of plywood. What is its total surface area?

Answer:

QUESTION 6

A rectangular piece of plywood measures 1.55 m by 1.28 m. What is the total area of the plywood?

Answer:

QUESTION 7

The measurement of an access panel in a floor is 45 cm by 45 cm. What is the total area of the access panel?

Answer:

QUESTION 8

A storage area for timber is 65.3 m by 32.7 m. How much storage area is available?

Answer:

QUESTION 9

An apprentice plasterer plasters a wall which is 8.6 m long and 3.2 m wide.

Answer:

QUESTION 10

A company van that carries timber measures 8.9 m long and 2.6 m wide. How much floor area is there?

Answer:

Section D: Volume of a cuboid

Short-answer questions

Specific instructions to students

- This section is designed to help you both to improve your skills and to increase your speed in calculating the **volume** of cubes or cuboids.
- Read the following questions and answer all of them in the spaces provided.
- You need to show all working, you can use the blank Notes pages at the back of this book.

> Volume = length × width × height and is given in cubic units
>
> = $l \times w \times h$

QUESTION 1

How many cubic metres are there in a timber yard that has a storage rack that measures 13 m by 5 m by 4 m?

Answer:

QUESTION 2

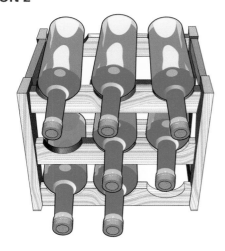

A wine rack is made with the following dimensions: 2 m × 1 m × 0.5 m. What is the wine rack's volume?

Answer:

QUESTION 3

A builder builds a room in a house that measures 3 m long by 2 m high by 3 m wide. How many cubic metres of volume does this make?

Answer:

QUESTION 4

An apprentice constructs a wardrobe that measures 2.2 m × 1.8 m × 0.5 m. How much volume is available inside?

Answer:

QUESTION 5

A carpenter makes a wooden toy box with the dimensions 60 cm by 15 cm by 50 cm. How many cubic centimetres does the toy box contain?

Answer:

QUESTION 6

If a bathroom cabinet measures 1.2 m × 0.6 m × 0.25 m, what cubic area is available for storage inside it?

Answer:

QUESTION 7

A cabinet maker's toolbox is 50 cm long, 30 cm wide and 25 cm tall. How many cubic centimetres are available for storing tools inside it?

Answer:

QUESTION 8

The back of a delivery van is 1.4 m wide × 1.6 m long × 88 cm high. What is the volume of the boot? Give your answer in cubic centimetres and cubic metres.

Answer:

QUESTION 9

A builder plasterboards a wall that is 1.75 m high by 1.35 m wide by 3.6 m long. How many cubic metres of space is there in the shed?

Answer:

QUESTION 10

A carpenter has a room that measures 3.8 m by 3.8 m by 2.5 m. How many cubic metres are there for storage of the carpenter's tools?

Answer:

Section E: Volume of a cylinder

Short-answer questions

Specific instructions to students

- This section is designed to help you both to improve your skills and to increase your speed in calculating the volume of cylinders.
- Read the following questions and answer all of them in the spaces provided.
- You need to show all working, you can use the blank Notes pages at the back of this book.

> Volume of a cylinder (V_c) = π (3.14) × r^2 × height
> $V_c = π × r^2 × h$
> (r^2 = radius × radius)

QUESTION 1

What is the volume of a cylindrical concrete post that has a **radius** of 13 cm and a height of 90 cm?

Answer:

QUESTION 2

What is the volume of a tube of liquid nails that has a radius of 3 cm and height of 25 cm?

Answer:

QUESTION 3

A can of primer has a radius of 4 cm and a height of 11 cm. What is its volume?

Answer:

QUESTION 4

A grease gun has a radius of 2.5 cm and a length of 28 cm. How much grease can it hold?

Answer:

QUESTION 5

A can of lubricant has a radius of 2.5 cm and a height of 16.5 cm. What is its volume?

Answer:

QUESTION 6

A painter and decorator buys a tub of acrylic caulk. If the cylinder has a radius of 5 cm and a height of 25 cm, what is the volume?

Answer:

QUESTION 7

A 4-litre container of mineral turpentine gets poured into 3 cylinders. Each cylinder has a radius of 4.5 cm and a height of 20 cm.

a   What is the volume of each container?

Answer:

_____

b   What is the volume of all 3 containers in total?

Answer:

_____

c   How much is left in the 4 litre container?

Answer:

_____

QUESTION 8

A container of linseed putty has a radius of 10.5 cm and a height of 15 cm.

a   What is its volume?

Answer:

_____

b   If you use exactly half on one job, how much is left?

Answer:

_____

QUESTION 9

A can of general purpose thinners has a radius of 11.7 cm and a height of 22.4 cm.

a   What is its volume?

Answer:

_____

b   If you use 750 ml, how much is left?

Answer:

_____

QUESTION 10

An apprentice uses a can of masonry paint that has a radius of 6 cm and a height of 18 cm. What is its volume?

Answer:

_____

Unit 15: Earning Wages

Short-answer questions

Specific instructions to students

- This unit will help you to calculate how much a job is worth, and how long you need to complete the job.
- Read the following questions and answer all of them in the spaces provided.
- You need to show all working, you can use the blank Notes pages at the back of this book.

QUESTION 1

A first-year carpentry apprentice earns £250.40 after tax per week. How much has she earned after tax per year?

Answer:

QUESTION 2

Paul the apprentice wall tiler starts work at 7.00 a.m. and stops for a break at 9.30 a.m. for 20 minutes. Lunch is at 1.15 p.m. for 45 minutes and then he works through to 4.00 p.m. How many hours has he worked for, excluding breaks?

Answer:

QUESTION 3

A cabinet maker earns £35.00 an hour and works a 38-hour week. How much is his gross earnings (before tax)?

Answer:

QUESTION 4

Over a week, an apprentice completes 5 jobs. The cost of each job is as follows: £465.80, £2490.50, £556.20, £1560.70 and £990.60. What is the total cost for all of the jobs?

Answer:

QUESTION 5

A builder takes 34 minutes to construct a window frame, 8 minutes to cut three lengths of timber and 27 minutes to construct a door frame. How much time has been worked in total on this job? State your answer in hours and minutes.

Answer:

QUESTION 6

A house is being renovated. On the first day Raj the joiner takes 4½ hours removing the old floorboards from the ground floor. If his rate of pay is £28.60 per hour, how much has Raj earned?

Answer:

QUESTION 7

An apprentice takes 1½ hours to complete the installation of a new window frame. If the apprentice is getting paid £9.80 per hour, what are his total earnings?

Answer:

QUESTION 8

The roof on a house suffers storm damage and needs repairing. The joiner spends 116 hours carrying out the repairs. If he worked 8 hours per day, how many days did the repairs take to complete?

Answer:

QUESTION 9

An apprentice begins work at 7.00 a.m. and works until 3.30 p.m. The morning break lasts for 20 minutes, the lunch break goes for 60 minutes and the afternoon break lasts 20 minutes.

a   How much time has been spent on breaks?

Answer:

---

b   How much time has been spent working?

Answer:

QUESTION 10

The cost of labour on a renovation job is £960.00. The builder spends 24 hours on the job. How much is the rate of pay per hour?

Answer:

QUESTION 11

A bricklaying team works on a self-employed basis. When they take on a contract they need to work out how much each member of the team will earn and how much this is each week. Study the advert below and answer the questions.

> ### Bricklaying Team Wanted
>
> Large contract in the NW of England worth: £11,700
>
> Contract time: 5 weeks
>
> We are looking for a reliable three-man bricklaying team to fulfil the above contract. All applicants must be fully trained and able to work as a team. For further details please contact:
>
> Martin Jones
>
> Able Contracts
>
> Blackpool, England
>
> Tel: 09997 5543001

a   How much can the team expect to earn each week?

Answer:

---

b   If they share out the wages equally, how much will each bricklayer earn for 5 weeks work?

Answer:

---

c   If they share the money out equally, how much will each bricklayer earn each week?

Answer:

---

d   The team decides to pay a labourer £300.00 per week for five weeks. How much will the labourer earn?

Answer:

Unit 16: Squaring Numbers

Section A: Introducing square numbers

Short-answer questions

Specific instructions to students

- This section is designed to help you both to improve your skills and to increase your speed in squaring numbers.
- Read the following questions and answer all of them in the spaces provided.
- You need to show all working, you can use the blank Notes pages at the back of this book.

> Any number squared is multiplied by itself.

EXAMPLE

4 squared $= 4^2 = 4 \times 4 = 16$

QUESTION 1

$6^2 =$

Answer:

QUESTION 2

$8^2 =$

Answer:

QUESTION 3

$12^2 =$

Answer:

QUESTION 4

$3^2 =$

Answer:

QUESTION 5

$7^2 =$

Answer:

QUESTION 6

$11^2 =$

Answer:

QUESTION 7

$10^2 =$

Answer:

QUESTION 8

$9^2 =$

Answer:

QUESTION 9

$2^2 =$

Answer:

QUESTION 10

$4^2 =$

Answer:

QUESTION 11

$5^2 =$

Answer:

Section B: Applying square numbers to the trade

Worded practical problems

Specific instructions to students

- This section is designed to help you to both improve your skills and to increase your speed in calculating the area of rectangular or square objects. The worded questions make the content relevant to everyday situations.
- Read the following questions and answer all of them in the spaces provided.
- You need to show all working, you can use the blank Notes pages at the back of this book.

QUESTION 1

An apprentice sets aside an area to cut timber. The area measures 2.8 m × 2.8 m. What is the area in square metres?

Answer:

QUESTION 2

A carpentry workshop has a work area that is 5.2 m × 5.2 m. What is the total area?

Answer:

QUESTION 3

The dimensions of a kitchen are 2.6 m × 2.6 m. What is the total area?

Answer:

QUESTION 4

An apprentice works in an area that is 15 m × 15 m. If there is an area allocated for storage that is 2.4 m × 2.4 m, how much area is left for the apprentice to work in?

Answer:

QUESTION 5

A joiner's workshop has a total floor area of 13.8 m × 13.8 m. The workbench area takes up 1.2 m × 1.2 m and the timber storage area is 2.7 m × 2.7 m. How much area is left to work in?

Answer:

QUESTION 6

A carpenter has a sheet of MDF that measures 2.4 m × 2.4 m. If 1.65 m × 1.65 m is cut out of it, how much is left?

Answer:

QUESTION 7

An apprentice cuts out a piece of aquaboard for a wet room that measures 50 cm × 50 cm from a sheet that is 120 cm × 120 cm. What area is left?

Answer:

QUESTION 8

A workshop floor measures 28.2 m × 28.2 m. If it costs £9.50 to seal 1 m², how much will it cost to seal the whole floor?

Answer:

_____

_____

QUESTION 9

A builder wants to insulate the four walls of a bedroom. Each wall measures 2.6 m × 2.6 m. It costs £28.50 to insulate 1 m².

a How much will it cost to insulate 1 wall?

Answer:

_____

b How much will it cost to insulate all 4 walls?

Answer:

_____

QUESTION 10

A cabinet maker cuts a 1150 mm × 1150 mm piece from a sheet of MDF. What is the total area of the cut piece?

Answer:

_____

Unit 17: Ratios and Averages

Section A: Introducing ratios L1 L2

Short-answer questions

Specific instructions to students

- This section is designed to help to improve your skills in calculating and simplifying ratios.
- Read the following questions and answer all of them in the spaces provided.
- You need to show all working, you can use the blank Notes pages at the back of this book.
- Reduce the ratios to the simplest or lowest form.

QUESTION 1

The number of teeth on gear cog A is 40. The number of teeth on gear cog B is 20. What is the ratio of gear cog A to gear cog B?

Answer:

_____

QUESTION 2

Cutting disc A has a diameter of 48 cm and cutting disc B has a diameter of 16 cm. What is the ratio of diameter A to B?

Answer:

_____

QUESTION 3

Cutting disc A has a diameter of 48 cm and cutting disc B has a diameter of 16 cm. What is the ratio of diameter A to B?

Answer:

_____

QUESTION 4

Two hand saws have 300 and 60 teeth respectively. What is the ratio of the teeth?

Answer:

_____

QUESTION 5

Three building companies employ 80, 60 and 20 people. what is the ratio of employees?

Answer:

_____

QUESTION 6

A lathe has 2 pulleys that have diameters of 16 cm and 20 cm respectively. What is the ratio?

Answer:

_____

QUESTION 7

The diameter of pulley A on a band saw is 32 cm. Pulley B has a diameter of 16 cm and pulley C has a diameter of 48 cm. Write the ratio of the diameters.

Answer:

_____

QUESTION 8

Three tins of paint have different diameters: 18 cm, 16 cm and 10 cm respectively. What is the comparative ratio?

Answer:

_____

QUESTION 9

Diamond core drill A has a diameter of 34 cm and diamond core drill B has a diameter of 12 cm. What is the ratio of the diameters A : B?

Answer:

QUESTION 10

The circumference of hole saw A is 62 cm and the circumference of hole saw B is 38 cm. What is the ratio of the circumferences?

Answer:

Section B: Applying ratios to the trade

Short-answer questions

Specific instructions to students

- This section is designed to help to improve your practical skills when working with ratios.
- Read the following questions and answer all of them in the spaces provided.
- You need to show all working, you can use the blank Notes pages at the back of this book.

QUESTION 1

The ratio of the teeth on cog 1 to cog 2 is 3 : 1. If cog 2 has 10 teeth, how many teeth will cog 1 have?

Answer:

QUESTION 2

The ratio of the teeth on hand saw 1 to hand saw 2 is 2 : 1. If hand saw 2 has 20 teeth, how many teeth will hand saw 1 have?

Answer:

QUESTION 3

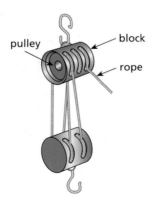

pulley   block

rope

The ratio of the diameter of pulley A to pulley B is 4 : 3. If pulley A has a diameter of 40 cm, what will be the diameter of pulley B?

Answer:

QUESTION 4

The ratio of the diameter of pulley A to pulley B is 2 : 1. If pulley A has a diameter of 30 cm, what will be the diameter of pulley B?

Answer:

QUESTION 5

The ratio of teeth on hole saw A to hole saw B is 3 : 1. If the number of teeth on hole saw A is 120, how many teeth are on hole saw B?

Answer:

QUESTION 6

The ratio of teeth on circular saws A to B is 2 : 1. If the number of teeth on circular saw A is 180, How many teeth are on circular saw B?

Answer:

QUESTION 7

The ratio of teeth on jigsaw A to jigsaw B is 3 : 1. If the number of teeth on jigsaw A is 21, how many teeth are on jigsaw B?

Answer:

QUESTION 8

The ratio of teeth on circular saw A to circular saw B is 3 : 2. If the number of teeth on circular saw A is 60, how many teeth are on circular saw B?

Answer:

QUESTION 9

The ratio of teeth on cog A to cog B is 4 : 3. If the number of teeth on cog A is 16, how many teeth will be on cog B?

Answer:

QUESTION 10

The ratio of teeth on hand saw A to hand saw B is 4 : 3. If the number of teeth on hand saw A is 24, how many teeth will be on hand saw B?

Answer:

Section C: Mean, median, mode and range

Short-answer questions

Specific instructions to students

- This section will help you improve your skills when working with averages.
- The **mean**, **median**, **range** and **mode** are all types of average. Read the definitions, study the examples and then complete the table.
- You need to show all working, you can use the blank Notes pages at the back of this book.

Definition	Example series: 2, 2, 4, 4, 6, 8, 10, 12	Find the averages for the following series: 4, 4, 6, 10, 12, 14, 16, 18, 20, 20
THE MEAN To find the mean, you need to add up all the data, and then divide this total by the number of values in the data set.	Adding the numbers up gives: $2+2+4+4+6+8+10+12 = 52$ There are 8 values, so divide the total by 8: $52 \div 8 = 6.5$ **So the mean is 6.5**	
THE MEDIAN To find the median, you need to put the values in order, and then find the middle value. If there are two values in the middle then you find the mean of these two values.	The numbers in order 2,2,4,**4**,**6**,8,10,12 The middle value are in bold $4 + 6 = 10$ $10 \div 2 = 5$ **So the median is 5**	
THE MODE The mode is the value that appears the most often in the data. It is possible to have more than one mode if there is more than one value that appears the most.	The data values 2,2,4,4,6,8,10,12 The values that appear most often are 2 and 4. They both appear more times than any other data values. **So the modes are 2 and 4**	
THE RANGE To find the range, you first need to find the lowest and highest values in the data. The range is found by subtracting the lowest value from the highest value.	The data values 2,2,4,4,6,8,10,12 The lowest value is 2 and the highest value is 12. $12 - 2 = 10$ **So the range is 10**	

Unit 18: Pythagoras' Theorem

Short-answer questions

Specific instructions to students

- This section is designed to help to improve your skills in calculating measurement and area using Pythagoras' theorem.
- Read the following questions and answer all of them in the spaces provided.
- You need to show all working, you can use the blank Notes pages at the back of this book.

Pythagoras' theorem applies to right-angled triangles, which are often found in the building and carpentry industry.

$$a^2 + b^2 = c^2$$

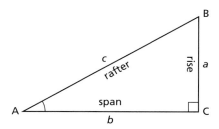

To solve for c, you need to find the square root of $a^2 + b^2$, that is $\sqrt{(a^2 + b^2)}$

If we consider this formula as it applies to the building trade, we can introduce the following terms specifically when considering rafters — the main structural roof supports.

a = rise (the change in roof elevation)

b = span (the horizontal distance between the rafter and the rise)

c = diagonal length of the rafter

To find c, or the length of the rafter, you can use the formula:

$$\text{rise}^2 + \text{span}^2 = \text{rafter}^2$$

To solve Questions 1–3, you will need to refer to the following example.

EXAMPLE

If the rise measures 2 m and the span is 4 m, what is the diagonal length of the rafter (c)?

$$\text{rise}^2 + \text{span}^2 = \text{rafter}^2$$
$$2^2 + 4^2 = c^2$$
$$4 + 16 = c^2$$
$$20 = c^2$$
$$\sqrt{20} = c$$
$$4.47 = c$$

Therefore, c, the diagonal length of the rafter or roof, is 4.47 m.

QUESTION 1

If the rise is 3 m and the span is 3 m, what is the diagonal length of the rafter?

Answer:

QUESTION 2

If the rise is 2.1 m and the span is 2.5 m, what is the diagonal length of the rafter?

Answer:

QUESTION 3

If the rise is 2.5 m and the span 4 m, what is the diagonal length of the rafter?

Answer:

To solve Questions 4–6, you will need to refer to the following example.

> ### EXAMPLE
>
> If you know the rise and the diagonal length of the rafter but need to calculate its span, you can subtract the rise squared from the square of the diagonal length of the rafter:
>
> span^2 = diagonal length of the rafter^2 − rise^2
>
>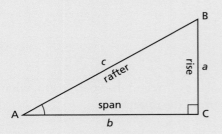
>
> If the diagonal length of the rafter is 5 m and the rise is 2 m, what is the span?
>
> span^2 = rafter^2 − rise^2
> span^2 = 5^2 − 2^2
> span^2 = 25 − 4
> span^2 = 21
> span = √21
> span = 4.58
>
> Therefore, the span is 4.58 m long.

QUESTION 4

If the diagonal length of the rafter is 4 m and the rise is 3 m, what length is the span?

Answer:

_____

QUESTION 5

If the diagonal length of the rafter is 3.8 m and the rise is 2.2 m, what length is the span?

Answer:

_____

QUESTION 6

If the diagonal length of the rafter is 3.5 m and the rise 1.5 m, what length is the span?

Answer:

_____

To solve Questions 7–9, you will need to refer to the following example.

_____

> ### EXAMPLE
>
> If you know the span and the diagonal length of the rafter and need to calculate the rise, you can subtract the span squared from the square of the diagonal length of the rafter:
>
> rise^2 = diagonal length of the rafter^2 − span^2
>
> If the span is 3 m and the diagonal length of the rafter is 4 m, what is the rise?
>
> rise^2 = rafter^2 − span^2
> rise^2 = 4^2 − 3^2
> rise^2 = 16 − 9
> rise^2 = 5
> rise = √5
> rise = 2.23
>
> Therefore, the rise is 2.23 m long.

QUESTION 7

If the diagonal length of the rafter is 5 m and the span is 4 m, what is the rise?

Answer:

_____

QUESTION 8

If the diagonal length of the rafter is 8 m and the span is 6 m, what is the rise?

Answer:

_____

QUESTION 9

If the diagonal length of the rafter is 7 m and the span 6 m, what is the rise?

Answer:

_____

Short-answer questions

Specific instructions to students

- This section is designed to help to improve your skills in calculating measurements using trigonometry.
- Read the following questions and answer all of them in the spaces provided.
- You need to show all working, you can use the blank Notes pages at the back of this book.

Trigonometry can often be used in building to determine measurements and angles. It is particularly useful when trying to find an unknown length.

Trigonometry can be used in conjunction with Pythagoras' theorem: together, they can solve nearly all problems that a builder will come across when using right-angled triangles.

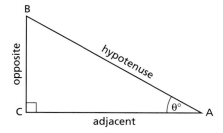

The following rules can be applied to the above triangle.

Rule 1

$$\sin \theta° = \frac{\text{length of opposite side}}{\text{length of hypotenuse side}} = \frac{\text{opp}}{\text{hyp}}$$

Rule 2

$$\cos \theta° = \frac{\text{length of adjacent side}}{\text{length of hypotenuse side}} = \frac{\text{adj}}{\text{hyp}}$$

Rule 3

$$\tan \theta° = \frac{\text{length of opposite side}}{\text{length of adjacent side}} = \frac{\text{opp}}{\text{adj}}$$

The name of each side is determined by the location of the angle in the triangle.

EXAMPLE

If the diagonal length of a rafter is 10 m and the angle that the rafter makes with the span is 27°, find the height of the rise and the length of the span? (Hint: draw a diagram to illustrate the problem, and then use sin and cos to solve it.)

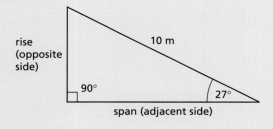

To find the rise:

$$\sin 27° = \frac{\text{rise}}{10}$$

$$\sin 27° \times 10 = \text{rise}$$

Using a calculator, $\sin 27° = 0.4539$

So $0.4539 \times 10 = 4.54$

Therefore, the height of the rise is 4.54 m.

To find the span:

$$\cos 27° = \frac{\text{span}}{10}$$

$$\cos 27° \times 10 = \text{span}$$

Using a calculator, $\cos 27° = 0.891$

So, $0.8910 \times 10 = 8.91$

Therefore, the length of the span is 8.91 m.

Solve the following by first drawing a diagram to illustrate each problem and then using sin and cos.

QUESTION 1

If the diagonal length of a roof is 5 m and the angle that the roof makes with the span is 21°, find the height of the rise and the length of the span.

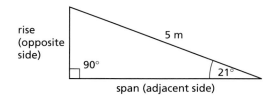

Answer:

_____

QUESTION 2

If the diagonal length of a roof is 8000 mm and the angle that the roof makes with the span is 25°, find the height of the rise and the length of the span.

Answer:

QUESTION 3

If the diagonal length of a rafter is 11 m and the angle that the roof makes with the span is 27°, find the height of the rise and the length of the span.

Answer:

In a rafter construction job, the angle that a rafter makes with the span is 25°. The length of the span is 4 m. Calculate the rise and diagonal length of the rafters on each side of the roof. (Remember to make a right angle in your drawing before you begin.)

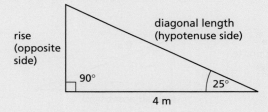

To find the diagonal length of the rafter:

$$\cos 25° = \frac{4}{\text{diagonal length}}$$
$$\text{diagonal length} = \frac{4}{\cos 25°}$$
$$\text{diagonal length} = \frac{4}{0.9063}$$
$$\text{diagonal length} = 4.41 \text{ m}$$

Therefore, the diagonal length of the rafter is 4.41 m.

To find the rise:
$$\sin 25° = \frac{\text{rise}}{4.41}$$
$$\sin 25° \times 4.41 = \text{rise}$$
$$0.4226 \times 4.41 = \text{rise}$$
$$1.86 = \text{rise}$$

Therefore, the height of the rise is 1.86 m.

Solve the following by first drawing a diagram to illustrate each problem and then using sin, cos or tan.

QUESTION 4

If the total length of the span is 4 m and the angle that the rafter makes with the span is 28° on both sides, find the diagonal length of the rafters of the roof and the rise.

Answer:

QUESTION 5

If the total length of the span is 10 m and the angle that the rafter makes with the span is 23° on both sides, find the diagonal length of the rafters and the rise.

Answer:

QUESTION 6

If the total length of the span is 9 m and the angle that the rafter makes with the span is 25° on both sides, find the diagonal length of the rafters and the rise.

Answer:

Short-answer questions

Specific instructions to students

- This section is designed to help to improve your skills in mechanical reasoning.
- Read the following questions and answer all of them in the spaces provided.
- You need to show all working, you can use the blank Notes pages at the back of this book.

QUESTION 1

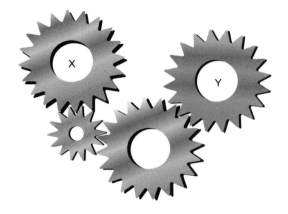

If cog X turns in a clockwise direction, which way will cog Y turn?

Answer:

_____

QUESTION 2

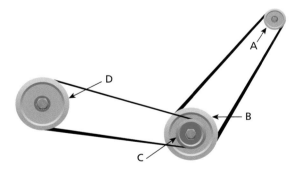

If pulley A turns in a clockwise direction, which way will pulley D turn?

Answer:

_____

QUESTION 3

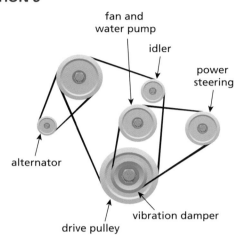

If the drive pulley in a work van engine turns in a clockwise direction, in which direction will the alternator turn?

Answer:

_____

QUESTION 4

Looking at the following diagram, if lever A moves to the left, in which direction will lever B move?

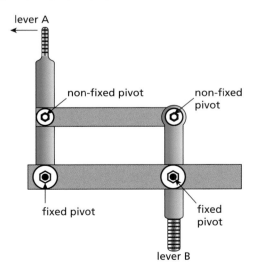

Answer:

_____

QUESTION 5

In the following diagram, pulley 1 turns clockwise. In what direction will pulley 6 turn?

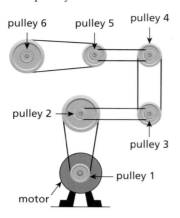

Answer:

QUESTION 6

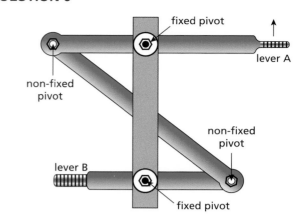

If lever A is pulled up, what will happen to lever B?

Answer:

Unit 21: Reading, Interpreting and Understanding Information in Charts and Graphs L1 L2

The Health and Safety at Work Act 1974 is the principal piece of legislation covering work-based health and safety requirements. Below is a chart showing the most common types of work-based injuries. From the given data answer the following questions.

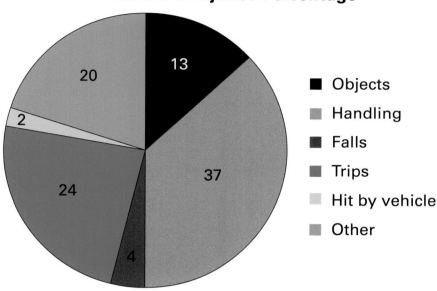

Causes of Injuries Percentage

- Objects
- Handling
- Falls
- Trips
- Hit by vehicle
- Other

QUESTION 1

What is the name given to the above type of chart?

Answer:

_____

QUESTION 2

What is the most common cause of injuries?

Answer:

_____

QUESTION 3

What percentage of injuries does the most common cause make up?

Answer:

_____

QUESTION 4

What percentage of injuries is caused by trips?

Answer:

_____

QUESTION 5

20 percent of injuries are designated 'other'. Name some things you consider that 'other' could be.

Answer:

_____

QUESTION 6

Using the data above, draw a bar chart showing all the details.

Answer:

QUESTION 7

Using the data above, draw a line graph showing all the details and percentages.

Answer:

Unit 22:
Practice Written Exam for the Construction Multi-Skills Industry

Reading time: 10 minutes

Writing time: 1 hour 30 minutes

Section A: English

Section B: Mathematics

QUESTION and ANSWER BOOK

Section	Topic	Number of questions	Marks
A	English	10	90
B	Mathematics	21	70
		Total 31	Total 160

The sections may be completed in the order of your choice.

Task 1: Job application

10 marks

Brentwood Building Services

We require a decorator trainee to join our installation team!

Full training will be provided in all aspects of the decorating industry.

If you are looking to enter the decorating industry and are enthusiastic about the decorating industry, then do not hesitate contact us today!

Contact:
Alan Brentwood,
Brentwood Building Services,
106 Main Road Industrial Estate,
Leeds Road,
Newtown,
Lancashire OH5 7BD.

You have seen this advertisement in your local newspaper and you would like to apply for the trainee position. The company is well established and has an excellent reputation.

Write a letter of application to the company, providing full personal details. You should include:
- Why you would like to work for the company
- All relevant qualifications
- What experience you have; this could be any work experience or voluntary work
- What skills and experience you could bring to the company
- Why you want to be a decorator.

You should:
- Use the correct letter format
- Write in full sentences
- Use correct spelling, punctuation and grammar.

Remember: Plan your letter of application before you write your draft and final letter.

Answer:

Task 2: Car auction

10 marks

You are placing an advert on an auction website to sell your car. Write a full and honest description, highlighting all of the good points that will persuade someone to bid on your item. Think carefully about:
* The tone and language you use, to make your item sound appealing to potential customers
* Making sure your description is clear and concise
* The use of fact and opinion in your description.

Answer:

Task 3: Cover letter

Rhia has written in response to the advertisement that she spotted in her local newspaper, shown below.

Retail assistant

Required for local hardware store. Must have 2 years' experience.

Please send your CV and covering letter, to:

Jenny Clucas

Red34 at Ledbury

Harley Drive

Ledbury

She has asked you to look over her covering letter before she posts it to see if she has included all the relevant points. She has also asked if you can help her write it again, if necessary.

Hi there

I want the job you've put in the local newspaper this week. I've been in retail for 2 years and I can get people to vouch for me, if you want. Here's a list of my qualifications and where I've worked before, in with this letter.

You can call me on 07562 725094

Rhia

Help Rhia by rewriting the short covering letter to accompany her CV, using the correct structure, content and layout for a formal covering letter.

Answer:

Task 4: Flyers

Specialist Tool Centre
Crazy! Crazy!
Spring sale!

The Specialist Tool Centre is leading the way in tool discount madness; yes, we are giving all our customers up to 30% discount on our full range of high quality power tools!

Yes, you will be amazed at how low our prices are for all, yes all, our latest high quality battery drills, impact drivers, diamond core drills, core drills and many, many more items!

You will be amazed, thrilled and staggered at how low our prices are; so don't delay! Come and visit us today.

Offer open for one week only!

Specialist Tool Centre, Unit 5 North Road Park, Elton, Lancashire.
Tel: 0164 755 67774
www.specialisttoolcentre.com

You have been given a flyer for the Specialist Tool Centre spring sale.

QUESTION 1
1 mark

Which of the following statements best describes the purpose of the flyer:
(1) To criticise
(2) To assess
(3) To advertise
(4) To review

Answer:

QUESTION 2
4 marks

The flyer has been designed to give maximum impact and promote the sale. List four high impact words used in the advertisement.

Answer:

You are the owner of a successful gardening business and would like to attract more customers. Produce a flyer for your business using high impact words to maximise the impact of the flyer.

Answer:

Task 5: Help from a friend

22 marks

You have set up as a self-employed builder and become successful. You now want to expand your business, but need some help.

Your task is to write an email to a friend asking for help distributing fliers to the local area (residential and business addresses).

Your friend's email address is bill.bailey@helpme.co.uk

It would be good to expand on the following points:
- Your reason for writing
- Why you are excited and what expanding the business will mean to you
- Details of what you want your friend to do
- Why you have chosen them to help you
- Making arrangements to meet up and discuss what you will do.

Answer:

Task 6: New home build

12 marks

Your local council is to have a meeting to decide if a large building company can be granted planning permission to build 150 new homes on green belt land in the community. If planning permission is granted, it will have an immediate impact on local resources such as schools and hospitals, and cause increases in traffic and pollution. There are no plans to improve any local services to accommodate the growth in the local population.

Your task is to write a formal letter to the local planning department to complain about the proposed new houses and their effect on the local community. The person to write to is: Michael Jones, Head of Planning, Planning House, Taylor Street, Newbury NN12 6TY.

In your letter, you must include the following points:
* The main issue
* Who will be affected
* The effect on the local community
* Why you want to oppose the new house build.

Answer:

MODERN FURNITURE LTD

Announce the opening of our brand new showroom on Bank Holiday Monday at 9am!

We have a large display of tables, chairs and beds for your delight!

Come and have a look around and be amazed at our low prices!!

22 Main Street, Southtown, Lancashire SHU 4RT

www.modernfurniture.com

Above is an advertisement for the opening of a new furniture showroom. Answer the following questions:

a   When will the new showroom open?

_____

b   What will be on display in the showroom?

_____

c   Why will customers be amazed?

_____

d   What time will the new showroom open?

_____

e   What is the company name?

_____

f   What is the company web address?

_____

Task 8: Trainee Carpenter L2

Job description

You will be working for an established building company. You will have the opportunity to train as an apprentice carpenter in a full-time role where you will perfume basic duties to begin with.

Your role will include:

- Attending training as required

- Helping a qualified carpenter on site

- Meeting and greeting customers

- Observing and learning

- Tidying the work area.

Working week

You will be required to work Monday–Friday and some Saturdays if required, with one day a week (Tuesday) attending college (39-hour week including training).

Training to be provided

You will receive high levels of training and support while on the job. You will be working towards the NVQ Level 2 apprenticeships in carpentry and joinery at a local college on a day-release basis undertaking theory and practical tuition. This will be in addition to on the job training with an experienced carpenter.

Qualifications required

Ideally candidates should have GCSE (or equivalent) Maths and English at minimum grade C or above, or Functional Skills in Maths and English Level 1. Candidates that have not achieved the entry-level requirements will be required to undertake an assessment interview, and it will only be on successful completion of the assessment that they will be accepted onto the course. All candidates will be required to undertake Functional Skills as part of the training to a minimum of Level 1.

Skills required

Good communication skills and ability to work in a team. Candidates should be able to interact with both staff and customers.

Personal qualities required

Pleasant and honest disposition, as you will be dealing with the general public.

a   According to the text, which day is spent at college?

Answer:

_____

b   According to the text, what other day may have to be worked?

Answer:

_____

c   Name three basic duties required to be undertaken.

Answer:

_____

_____

_____

d   Using a dictionary, explain these words: *Communication, Interact, Apprentice, Assessment.*

Answer:

_____

_____

_____

_____

_____

_____

_____

_____

e   What qualifications are ideal for the job?

Answer:

_____

_____

f   What skills are required for the job?

Answer:

_____

_____

g   How many days a week would be spent at College?

Answer:

_____

h   What qualifications will be undertaken while at College?

Answer:

_____

_____

Section B: Mathematics

Task 1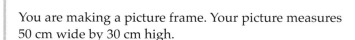

You are planning a kitchen. You work for a large kitchen design company and a customer wants some new kitchen units along one wall at home. You have to make a scale drawing for the customer.

The customer's wall is 3.5 m wide and 2.75 m high. You will draw a scale plan on graph paper where 4 cm represent 1 m.

QUESTION 1   2 marks

Work out the measurements for the plan. Show your working out.

Answer:

_____

_____

QUESTION 2   2 marks

Use the graph paper to draw a scale plan of the wall using the graph paper provided.

Answer:

_____

The wall units are 500 mm long × 750 mm high × 300 mm deep.

The base units are 500 mm long × 1000 mm high × 580 mm deep.

There is a tall fridge-freezer measuring 1500 mm high × 800 mm wide to be placed in the left-hand corner of the wall. Units are to be placed along the rest of the wall. The base units don't have any space between them, and neither do the wall units.

QUESTION 3   3 marks

Work out the maximum number of base units and maximum number of wall units. Each wall unit must be directly above a base unit. What is the width of the gap next to the fridge-freezer and cupboards? Show your working out.

Answer:

_____

_____

_____

QUESTION 4   6 marks

There should be a gap of 50 cm/500 mm between the wall units and base units. Draw the base units and the wall units on the scale diagram. Mark the space for the fridge freezer and label the diagram clearly showing the wall and base units and the fridge freezer.

Answer:

_____

_____

_____

QUESTION 5   2 marks

Double-check one of your calculations and show your working out.

Answer:

_____

Task 2

You are making a picture frame. Your picture measures 50 cm wide by 30 cm high.

QUESTION 1   2 marks

Draw a sketch using a suitable scale, clearly labelling the dimensions.

Answer:

_____

_____

_____

You will make the frame from four pieces of wood cut from one long strip. The strip of wood is 2.8 m (280 cm) long.

For the top and bottom of the frame you will need two pieces of wood cut to size in cm.

For the sides of the frame you will need to cut two pieces of wood to size in cm.

QUESTION 2   3 marks

Work out the sizes of the four pieces of wood that make up the picture frame. Show your working out.

Answer:

_____

_____

_____

_____

QUESTION 3   3 marks

How much wood will you have left over from your original strip? Show your working out.

Answer:

_____

_____

_____

QUESTION 4   5 marks

Draw a diagram on the graph paper to show where you will cut the long strip of wood to make four pieces of wood that make your picture frame. Each square on the graph paper is equal to 20 cm drawn to scale.

Answer:

_____

_____

_____

_____

_____

_____

_____

_____

_____

_____

QUESTION 5   2 marks

Check one of your calculations using repeat or reverse calculation methods and show your working out.

Answer:

_____

_____

Task 3 L2

You are planning a summer house for a garden. You work for a company that makes and sells summer houses. A customer wants a summer house and has asked that you build some decking on which to put the summer house in his garden.

The summer house measures 3600 mm long × 2400 mm wide. The decking that the customer has requested must have a border of 1500 mm framing the summer house.

QUESTION 1   3 marks

What are the dimensions of the decking? Show your working out.

Answer:

_____

_____

QUESTION 2   10 marks

The customer wants the decking and the summer house in the top right-hand corner of the gardens with the doors facing south. You must draw a scale plan to show the outline of the customer's garden. Add the decking and the summer house, to scale, onto your plan.

Use a suitable scale and label your diagram using the graph paper provided.

Answer:

_____

_____

_____

_____

_____

_____

_____

_____

_____

_____

_____

QUESTION 3 — 3 marks

What is the area of the decking you need for your customer? Show your working out.

Answer:

_____

_____

QUESTION 4 — 2 marks

One pack of garden decking covers 13 m square. How many packs of decking do you need? Show your working out.

Answer:

_____

_____

QUESTION 5 — 2 marks

Check one of your calculations.

Answer:

_____

Task 4

This task is about the time that it takes two teams of joiners to complete their jobs on a given day.

You are the supervisor and have set a target of 6.1 hours per job for each team member. The teams recorded how long they took to complete their jobs and the information is as follows:

Team 1		Team 2	
Bob	5.5 hrs	Luke	5.75 hrs
Bill	1.5 hrs	Chris	6.5 hrs
Eddie	6 hrs 30 mins	George	9 hrs
Harry	7 hrs 30 mins	Tyler	9 hrs 30 mins
Larry	6 hrs 10 mins	Richard	8 hrs
Tommy	6 hrs 50 mins	Bradley	5 hrs 15 mins
Nathan	3.5 hrs	Peter	8 hrs 45 mins
Charlie	6 hrs 30 mins	Ken	7 hrs 10 mins
		Alex	5 hrs 50 mins
		Sam	7.25 hrs

QUESTION 1 — 3 marks

What percentage of joiners spends more than 6.1 hours completing jobs? Show your working out.

Answer:

_____

QUESTION 2 — 5 marks

What are the mean numbers of hours spent completing jobs for the following? Show your answers in decimal format, not in time format. Show your working out.

Answer:

_____

_____

_____

QUESTION 3 — 5 marks

Draw a suitable chart on the graph paper provided on page 82 to show the mean numbers of hours spent completing jobs for Team 1, Team 2 and the combined teams, and also show the target set of 6.1 hours.

Answer:

_____

_____

_____

_____

_____

_____

QUESTION 4 — 3 marks

What is the range of times spent completing jobs for the following? Show your working out and give your answers in decimal format.

Answer:

_____

_____

_____

QUESTION 5   2 marks

Comment on the results of the survey and the target set for completing jobs. Include one comment about the mean numbers and one comment about the ranges.

Answer:

_____

_____

_____

_____

_____

_____

_____

QUESTION 6   2 marks

Check one of your calculations using reverse calculation method. Show your working out.

Answer:

_____

_____

_____

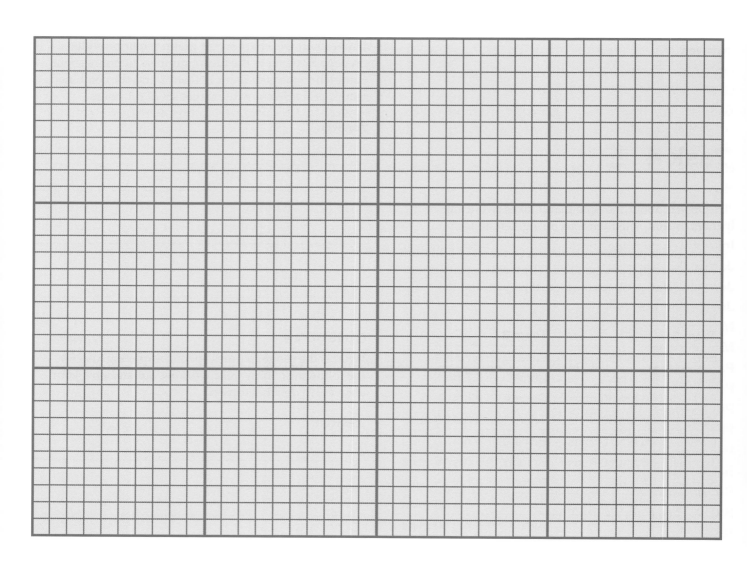

Construction Multi-Skills Glossary

Beam   A term used for joists, girders or rafters

Casing   The trim around a door or window, either outside or inside

Circumference   The perimeter of a circle

Civil engineering   The design and construction of things like roads, bridges and tunnels

Commercial   Relating to business that makes a profit – shops, showrooms and offices

Cornice   The exterior trim from the top of the wall to the projection of the rafters or the ceiling

Diameter   A line passing through the centre of a circle, extending from one side of the circumference to the other

Drywall   A wall covering of gypsum board

Environmental   To do with the natural world around us and our impact on it

Estimate   A costing for a piece of work that is not a fixed price but can go up or down

Executive   Someone who works in administration or management in a business

Fascia   A board that is nailed to the ends of the rafters

Flashing   Any material that is used around chimneys, vents and windows that prevents moisture from entering the building

Flush   Two members that form a level surface

Footing   Enlargement at the base of a column or a foundation wall

Foundation   The supporting structure found below grade. It is comprised of the footing with the foundation wall

Gable roof   A roof formed by universal rafters; it slopes up from two walls

Gusset   A bracket or panel that could be made of wood or metal that is attached to the corners of a frame to provide additional strength

Hazardous waste   Any waste materials on a building site that could be dangerous if not disposed of correctly

HSAWA 1974   Health and Safety at Work Act 1974 sets out safety rules for both employees and employers

HSE   Health and Safety Executive. This is the is the national independent watchdog for work-related health, safety and illness

Infrastructure   Network of services such as roads, power lines and water pipes

Invoice   A document used to show the cost and total amount of work completed

Jamb   The vertical posts that make up a window or doorframe

Joint   The place where two, or possibly more, members come together

Joist   This is a beam that can support a floor or ceiling

Masonry   Mortar bonds with materials to form a wall

Mortise   A hole or slot that a part or tenon may fit into

Particle board   A combination of woodchips and resin binder that are pressed into sheets that vary in thickness

Perimeter   The length of a boundary around a shape

Pitch (roof)   The incline of a roof as found by the rise divided by the span

PPE   Personal protective equipment. These are pieces of equipment worn to protect you against workplace hazards

Radius   The shortest distance from the centre of a circle to the circumference

Rafter   The main structural support of a roof

Refurbishment   Renewing the internal fittings, fixtures and finishes of a building

Ridge   The highest horizontal section of a roof

Rise   The change in elevation of a roof or stairs

Risk assessment   The detailed examination of any factors that could cause injury, to be carried out before starting work

Scaffold   A temporary platform that may be used to support both workers and/or equipment

Span   The distance between opposite sides of a building

Volt (V)   The unit of electrical potential or potential difference

Volume   The amount of space that a material occupies

English Glossary

Adjective   A type of word that describes NOUNS (things, people and places), for example *sharp*, *warm* or *handsome*.

Adverb   A type of word that describes VERBS (things happening), for example *slowly*, *often* or *quickly*.

Apostrophe   A PUNCTUATION mark with two main functions: (1) shows where letters have been missed out when words or phrases are shortened, for example changing *cannot* to *can't*, or *I will* to *I'll*; (2) shows where a NOUN 'possesses' something, for example *Dave's bike*, *the cat's whiskers* or *St John's Wood*.

Capital letter   Used to begin a SENTENCE, to begin the names of people, days, months and places, and for abbreviations such as *RSPCA* or *FBI*.

Comma   A PUNCTUATION mark that has many uses, usually to separate phrases in a long SENTENCE so that it is easier to read and understand, or to separate items in a list.

Formal language   The type of language used when speaking to or writing to someone you don't know, such as your bank manager (e.g. 'I am writing to request a bank statement').

Full stop   A PUNCTUATION mark used at the end of SENTENCES.

Future tense   The VERB forms we use to talk about things that will happen in future (e.g. 'I *will watch* television tonight').

Homophone   A word that sounds the same as another word, but has a different spelling and meaning, for example *break* and *brake*.

Informal language   The type of language used when you are speaking to or writing to someone you know well, such as a friend (e.g. 'Hi, how are you? Do you fancy coming to the cinema with me?').

Instructions   A series or list of statements designed to show someone how to do something, for example to use some equipment or to follow some rules.

Noun   A word used to refer to a thing, person or place, for example *chair*, *George* or *Sheffield*.

Paragraph   A section of writing about the same subject or topic, that begins on a new line and consists of one or more SENTENCES.

Past tense   The VERB forms we use to talk about things that have happened in the past (e.g. 'I *watched* television last night').

Present tense   The VERB forms we use to talk about things that are happening now (e.g. 'I *am watching* television').

Pronouns   Words that are used instead of NOUNS (things, people and places), for example *he*, *she*, *we*, *it*, *who*, *something*, *ourselves*.

Punctuation   Marks used in writing to help make it clear and organized, by separating or joining together words or phrases, or by adding or changing emphasis.

Question mark   A PUNCTUATION mark used at the end of a question, to show that you have asked something.

Sentence   A group of words, beginning with a CAPITAL LETTER and ending with a FULL STOP, QUESTION MARK or exclamation mark, put together using correct grammar, to make a meaningful statement or question, etc.

Verb   Word used to indicate an action, for example *mix*, *smile* or *walk*.

Mathematics Glossary

Actual   The exact calculation of a set of numbers.

Analogue clock   A clock that displays minute and hour hands and shows the time changing continuously.

Area   The size of a surface; the amount of space in a two-dimensional shape or property, e.g. the floor space of a room or flat.

Decimal   A way of organizing numbers based around the number ten (the most familiar system used in the world today).

Decimal point   A mark, often a full stop, used in a number to divide between whole numbers and FRACTIONS of whole numbers shown in DECIMAL form.

Digital clock   A clock that tells the time using numbers instead of hands and shows the time changing digitally – from one exact value to the next.

Estimate   (1) A calculation that requires a rough guess rather than working out the actual figure; (2) to work out this value.

Fraction   A quantity or amount that is not a whole number, e.g. less than 1. A part of a whole number.

Imperial   The British system of units for weights and measures before the METRIC system, including pounds, stones, miles, feet and inches.

Mean   A form of average of a set of numbers. To calculate the mean, add all of the numbers together and then divide by how many numbers there are.

Median   A form of average of a set of numbers. To calculate the median, place the numbers in numerical order and then find the middle number.

Metric   An international DECIMAL system of units for weights and measures, including kilograms, grams, kilometres, metres and centimetres.

Mode   A form of average of a set of numbers. To calculate the mode, look for the number that appears most often.

Percentage   A proportion, or FRACTION, that means part of one hundred.

Perimeter   The total lengths of all of the sides of a two-dimensional shape or AREA, e.g. the distance around the outside of a room.

Range   The difference between the largest and smallest numbers in a set of figures.

Ratio   A way to compare the amounts of things – how much of one thing there is compared to how much of another thing.

Scales   An instrument used to measure the weight of an object or person.

Volume   The amount of three-dimensional space that an object occupies.

Formulae and Data

Circumference of a Circle

$C = \pi \times d$
where: C = circumference, π = 3.14, d = diameter

Diameter of a Circle

Diameter (d) of a circle $= \dfrac{\text{circumference}}{\pi \ (3.14)}$

Area

Area = length $\times$ width (given in square units)
$\quad = l \times b$

Volume of a Cube

Volume = length $\times$ width $\times$ height (given in cubic units)
$\quad = l \times w \times h$

Volume of a Cylinder

Volume of a cylinder (V) = π (3.14) $\times r^2 \times$ height
$V = \pi \times r^2 \times h$

Pythagoras' Theorem

$a^2 + b^2 = c^2$

Trigonometry

Rule 1
$\sin \theta° = \dfrac{\text{length of opposite side}}{\text{length of hypotenuse side}} = \dfrac{\text{opp}}{\text{hyp}}$

Rule 2
$\cos \theta° = \dfrac{\text{length of adjacent side}}{\text{length of hypotenuse side}} = \dfrac{\text{adj}}{\text{hyp}}$

Rule 3
$\tan \theta° = \dfrac{\text{length of opposite side}}{\text{length of adjacent side}} = \dfrac{\text{opp}}{\text{adj}}$

Times Tables

1	**2**	**3**	**4**
1 × 1 = 1	1 × 2 = 2	1 × 3 = 3	1 × 4 = 4
2 × 1 = 2	2 × 2 = 4	2 × 3 = 6	2 × 4 = 8
3 × 1 = 3	3 × 2 = 6	3 × 3 = 9	3 × 4 = 12
4 × 1 = 4	4 × 2 = 8	4 × 3 = 12	4 × 4 = 16
5 × 1 = 5	5 × 2 = 10	5 × 3 = 15	5 × 4 = 20
6 × 1 = 6	6 × 2 = 12	6 × 3 = 18	6 × 4 = 24
7 × 1 = 7	7 × 2 = 14	7 × 3 = 21	7 × 4 = 28
8 × 1 = 8	8 × 2 = 16	8 × 3 = 24	8 × 4 = 32
9 × 1 = 9	9 × 2 = 18	9 × 3 = 27	9 × 4 = 36
10 × 1 = 10	10 × 2 = 20	10 × 3 = 30	10 × 4 = 40
11 × 1 = 11	11 × 2 = 22	11 × 3 = 33	11 × 4 = 44
12 × 1 = 12	12 × 2 = 24	12 × 3 = 36	12 × 4 = 48

5	**6**	**7**	**8**
1 × 5 = 5	1 × 6 = 6	1 × 7 = 7	1 × 8 = 8
2 × 5 = 10	2 × 6 = 12	2 × 7 = 14	2 × 8 = 16
3 × 5 = 15	3 × 6 = 18	3 × 7 = 21	3 × 8 = 24
4 × 5 = 20	4 × 6 = 24	4 × 7 = 28	4 × 8 = 32
5 × 5 = 25	5 × 6 = 30	5 × 7 = 35	5 × 8 = 40
6 × 5 = 30	6 × 6 = 36	6 × 7 = 42	6 × 8 = 48
7 × 5 = 35	7 × 6 = 42	7 × 7 = 49	7 × 8 = 56
8 × 5 = 40	8 × 6 = 48	8 × 7 = 56	8 × 8 = 64
9 × 5 = 45	9 × 6 = 54	9 × 7 = 63	9 × 8 = 72
10 × 5 = 50	10 × 6 = 60	10 × 7 = 70	10 × 8 = 80
11 × 5 = 55	11 × 6 = 66	11 × 7 = 77	11 × 8 = 88
12 × 5 = 60	12 × 6 = 72	12 × 7 = 84	12 × 8 = 96

9	**10**	**11**	**12**
1 × 9 = 9	1 × 10 = 10	1 × 11 = 11	1 × 12 = 12
2 × 9 = 18	2 × 10 = 20	2 × 11 = 22	2 × 12 = 24
3 × 9 = 27	3 × 10 = 30	3 × 11 = 33	3 × 12 = 36
4 × 9 = 36	4 × 10 = 40	4 × 11 = 44	4 × 12 = 48
5 × 9 = 45	5 × 10 = 50	5 × 11 = 55	5 × 12 = 60
6 × 9 = 54	6 × 10 = 60	6 × 11 = 66	6 × 12 = 72
7 × 9 = 63	7 × 10 = 70	7 × 11 = 77	7 × 12 = 84
8 × 9 = 72	8 × 10 = 80	8 × 11 = 88	8 × 12 = 96
9 × 9 = 81	9 × 10 = 90	9 × 11 = 99	9 × 12 = 108
10 × 9 = 90	10 × 10 = 100	10 × 11 = 110	10 × 12 = 120
11 × 9 = 99	11 × 10 = 110	11 × 11 = 121	11 × 12 = 132
12 × 9 = 108	12 × 10 = 120	12 × 11 = 132	12 × 12 = 144

Multiplication Grid

	1	2	3	4	5	6	7	8	9	10	11	12
1	1	2	3	4	5	6	7	8	9	10	11	12
2	2	4	6	8	10	12	14	16	18	20	22	24
3	3	6	9	12	15	18	21	24	27	30	33	36
4	4	8	12	16	20	24	28	32	36	40	44	48
5	5	10	15	20	25	30	35	40	45	50	55	60
6	6	12	18	24	30	36	42	48	54	60	66	72
7	7	14	21	28	35	42	49	56	63	70	77	84
8	8	16	24	32	40	48	56	64	72	80	88	96
9	9	18	27	36	45	54	63	72	81	90	99	108
10	10	20	30	40	50	60	70	80	90	100	110	120
11	11	22	33	44	55	66	77	88	99	110	121	132
12	12	24	36	48	60	72	84	96	108	120	132	144